Editor
Walter Kelly

Editorial Project Manager
Karen J. Goldfluss, M.S. Ed.

Editor-in-Chief
Sharon Coan, M.S. Ed.

Illustrator
Howard Chaney

Cover Artist
Sue Fullam

Art Director
Elayne Roberts

Associate Designer
Denise Bauer

Imaging
Ralph Olmedo, Jr.
Richard Yslava
James Edward Grace

Product Manager
Phil Garcia

Publishers
Rachelle Cracchiolo, M.S. Ed.
Mary Dupuy Smith, M.S. Ed.

JUMBO BOOK
of WRITING LESSONS

INTERMEDIATE

Authors

Marjorie Belshaw and *Dona Herweck Rice*

Teacher Created Materials, Inc.
6421 Industry Way
Westminster, CA 92683
www.teachercreated.com

©*1997 Teacher Created Materials, Inc.*
Reprinted, 2003
Made in U.S.A.
ISBN-1-57690-315-X

Table of Contents

Introduction

The *Jumbo Book of Writing Lessons* is designed to be used as a perpetual reference for all major writing skills necessary to become a good writer. This book is divided into two parts.

Part I

This section of the book contains lessons designed to guide students through the following writing topics:

- **Writing process**
- **Parts of speech**
- **Sensory words**
- **Exploring emotions**
- **Transition and sequential words**
- **Synonyms**
- **Homonyms**
- **Antonyms**
- **Similes and metaphors**
- **Idioms**
- **Alliteration**
- **Hyperbole**
- **Personification**
- **Unusual word combinations**
- **Writing sentences**
- **Writing paragraphs**
- **Quotations**
- **Writing stories**
- **Letter writing**
- **Contrast and comparison writing**
- **Point of view**
- **Opinions and editorials**
- **Summaries**
- **Interviews**
- **News reporting**
- **Book reports**
- **Outlines**
- **Applications**
- **Resumés**
- **Editing and proofreading**
- **Poetry**

Each lesson begins with a teacher guide page that sets the stage for the accompanying student pages. Space for additional teacher ideas or comments is provided on many teacher pages.

The lessons and worksheets developed in Part I should be implemented to reinforce, as well as to supplement, pages in the Writer's Notebook (Part II). Part I concludes with a number of writing prompt pages for additional writing practice.

Part II

This section is referred to as the Writer's Notebook. It contains examples, forms, rules, and other helpful information that support and reinforce the lessons in Part I. Writer's Notebook pages should be distributed to the students as personal references for writing skills. Students can keep their notebooks with them in the classroom and use them for homework assignments.

What Is the Writing Process?

The writing process is a natural procedure used by professional writers. It involves preparatory writing tasks, drafting, peer response, editing, revising, and publishing. These steps should be imitated by student writers since they dramatically improve the quality of completed writings. The steps are outlined below, and a student copy of the process can be found on page 2 of the Writer's Notebook.

I. Pre-writing

Pre-writing includes activities which procede and are preparatory to writing. They are necessary to most good writing. Activities include the following:

- Drawing/art
- Films
- Interviews
- Surveys
- Stories
- Observations
- Drama
- Patterning/modeling
- Discussions
- Mapping
- Brainstorming
- Outlining
- Clustering
- Questioning
- Dialogues
- Research

II. Writing

At this stage, pre-writing ideas take form as a rough draft. Writing activities include:

- Journals
- Learning logs
- Narratives
- Summaries
- Reports
- Lists
- Descriptions
- Stories
- Letters
- Notes
- Interviews
- Poems
- Skits and drama
- Speeches

III. Response

The writer can share with a peer what he has written in order to determine the clarity of his writing and to obtain suggestions for improvement. Response can be made by the student's teacher, partner, small group, or whole class.

IV. Revising

Revision includes consideration for the comments from the previous step as well as the writer's own judgment. Organization, clarity, unity, emphasis, and word selection should be considered. Most writing can—and should—be revised.

V. Editing

Editing is revision with a fine-tooth comb. It involves grammar and structure that conform to the standard rules of written language. Editing includes proofreading, sentence combining, and use of an editing checklist.

VI. Recopying

This is writing a final, proofread and edited draft.

VII. Publishing and Post-writing

This important step can take many forms, including illustrating, bookbinding, computer layout and graphics, displays, pen pals, class or school publications, awards, postings, group sharing, and contests.

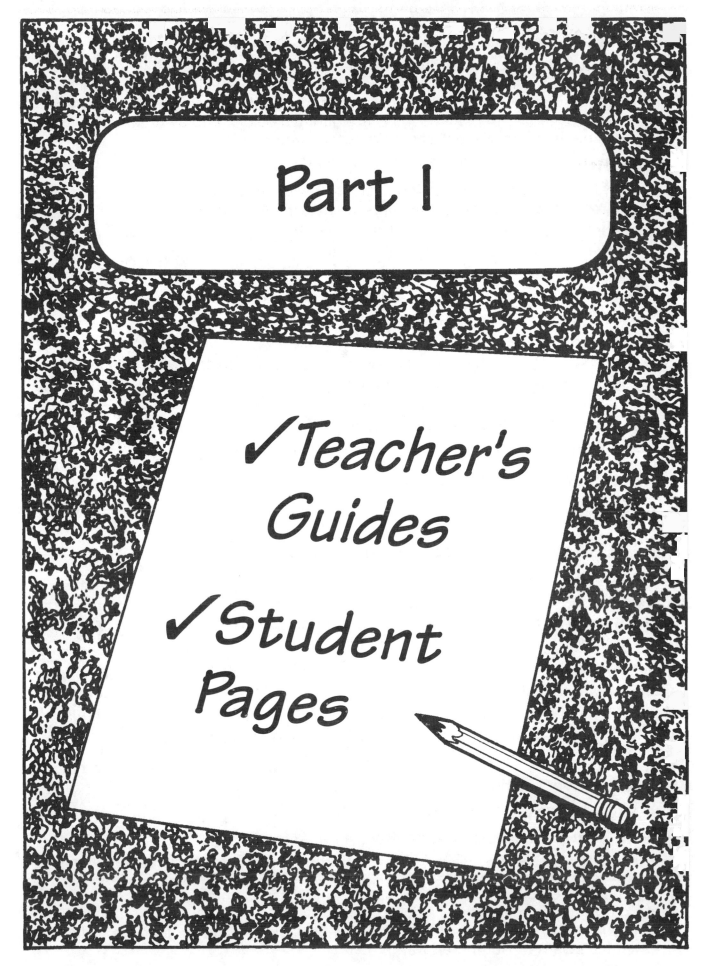

Part I

✓ Teacher's Guides

✓ Student Pages

Lesson 1—Parts of Speech

❑ Review the function of each part of speech.

noun: word that names a person, place, thing, or idea

pronoun: word used in place of a noun

verb: word that shows action or a state of being (existence)

adjective: word that describes a noun or pronoun

adverb: word that modifies a verb, adjective, or other adverb

preposition: word that shows how the object and another word are related

conjunction: word that connects other words or phrases

interjection: word used to show strong emotion

❑ Write a running list of each part of speech. Use pages 3–6 in the Writer's Notebook.

❑ Diagram sentences. Distribute Student Page 1 for students to complete alone or with partners. Page 7 in the Writer's Notebook shows proper form.

❑ Play Parts-of-Speech Bingo. Use Student Pages 2–7. To prepare, reproduce Student Pages 2–6. Cut out the sentences and place them together in a basket, jar, or small sack, mixing them well. Next, reproduce Student Page 7 so that each student can have a separate card. Fill in each space on the card with a letter, following these directions:

1. No two cards should be the same.

2. No two letters in one column should be the same.

3. The preposition column should not use the letters g, h, j, k, m, q, v, x, y, or z.

Laminate the cards for durability and cut them out. Then, collect a sizable number of durable markers so that each student can use approximately 25. Beans, seeds, unpopped popcorn, and paper clips make good markers.

To play, give each student a card and set of markers. Pull one sentence at a time from the bag. Read the italicized word and then read the sentence provided. Do not read the part of speech. If the student has the letter that begins the word in the column that says its part of speech, he can place a marker there. For example, if the word is "cat" and the sentence is "The cat purred," a student with a "c" in the noun column can place a marker in that space. Play for across, down, diagonal, or black-out. Remind the students to call out when they have a bingo match.

❑ Have the students write original sentences for Parts-of-Speech Bingo.

❑ Write parallel sentences. To do this, take sentences from published books and have the students write original sentences, mimicking the published sentence by each part of speech. For example, in Jean Craighead George's *My Side of the Mountain*, the author writes, "The sparrow flew across the meadow." The structure of the sentence is "adjective (article), noun, verb, preposition, adjective (article), noun (object of preposition). One possible parallel sentence is, "The crocodile swam through the swamp."

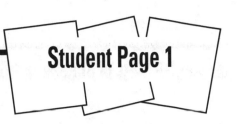

Lesson 1A—Sentence Diagrams

Directions: Diagram each of the sentences below.

1. The cat meowed.

2. The angry cat hissed.

3. The wild cat yowled fiercely.

4. The yellow cat sang through the night.

Noun How many *apples* do you have?	**Noun** A moonlit *night* is beautiful.
Noun The *boy* ran through the park.	**Noun** *Ostriches* can run very quickly.
Noun My sister got a pet *cat* for her birthday.	**Noun** The *poodle* looks small next to the Great Dane.
Noun Did you hear the *doorbell* ring just now?	**Noun** While the snow fell, the forest was filled with *quiet*.
Noun There were five *elephants* taking a bath in the tiny pool of water.	**Noun** The *radio* announced a contest today.
Noun My favorite *flower* is the yellow rose.	**Noun** How many houses are on your *street*?
Noun The *giant* ate three pies for dessert.	**Noun** The kitten got stuck in the highest branches of the *tree*.
Noun Can you do the *hula*?	**Noun** Just as the rain began to fall, my *umbrella* broke.
Noun The vanilla *ice cream* melted over the hot apple pie.	**Noun** Your *veins* carry blood to your heart.
Noun There was an old-fashioned *jukebox* at the school dance.	**Noun** Have you ever made a *wish* at a wishing well?
Noun The *kite* flew beyond the trees.	**Noun** The baby likes to play her toy *xylophone*.
Noun *Linda* laughed with all her friends.	**Noun** *Yellow* is my favorite color.
Noun The *mouse* ran away with the cheese.	**Noun** The strange zoo had *zebras* with purple stripes.

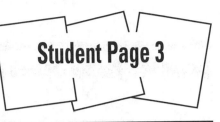

Verb He *ate* the cake himself.	**Verb** You *may go* to the party.
Verb When did you *buy* those shoes?	**Verb** I *noticed* your haircut the second I saw you.
Verb I *can go* to the movies, too.	**Verb** Please *open* the door.
Verb The children *dove* into the pool for a race.	**Verb** Who *put* that plate there?
Verb The clown *entertained* the crowd at the circus.	**Verb** The tired workers *quit* for the day.
Verb The pirate *was* sure to find the buried treasure.	**Verb** Who *can run* the fastest?
	Verb I do not know who *said* that.
Verb What gift *would* you *like* to give to your best friend.	**Verb** *Take* your place in line.
Verb I *hope* to see you at the party.	**Verb** I *understand.*
Verb The workers *ignited* the fireworks.	**Verb** *Be* sure to voice your opinion.
	Verb *Wait*!
Verb The angry crowd *jeered* at the fighting players.	**Verb** The technician *will x-ray* you now.
Verb He *kicked* the ball for the winning goal.	**Verb** The young children laughed and *yelled* as they played.
Verb *Did* you *look* at the rain clouds this morning?	**Verb** The red sports car *zipped* down the highway.

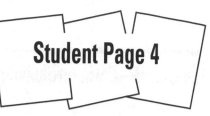

Preposition The children swam *across* the lake.

Preposition The puppies played *near* their mother.

Preposition The house sits *beyond* the trees.

Preposition Let's stop at the park *on* our way home from school.

Preposition I am calling you *concerning* our homework.

Preposition The baseball sailed *past* the shortstop and into the outfield.

Preposition My friend lives *down* the street.

Preposition *Regarding* our last conversation, I have changed my mind.

Preposition I like everything on my pizza *except* green peppers.

Preposition I have been waiting *since* nine o'clock.

Preposition This gift is *from* me to you.

Preposition Will you bring the box *to* me?

Preposition The wild coyote ran *into* the night.

Preposition We can easily put our meeting off *until* tomorrow.

Preposition *Like* me, he is wearing a blue baseball cap.

Preposition *With* a shout she slammed the door.

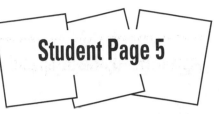
Adverb We *awkwardly* worked our way through the construction site.

Adverb The sun shone *brightly* through the clouds.

Adverb The basketball fell *cleanly* through the hoop.

Adverb The trapeze artist *daringly* leapt to her partner.

Adverb The basketball players were *extremely* tall.

Adverb The scent of *freshly* baked bread filled the house.

Adverb He *gingerly* stepped on the frozen pond.

Adverb The babies played *happily* together.

Adverb He answered my question *intelligently.*

Adverb *Joyfully,* the choir sang.

Adverb She *kindly* gave the family directions.

Adverb The lion *loudly* roared.

Adverb The butterflies fluttered *merrily* in the breeze.

Adverb The dogs barked *noisily.*

Adverb We go to the seashore *occasionally.*

Adverb I will bring the papers to you *presently.*

Adverb She *quickly* ran to the bus stop.

Adverb Do not eat *rapidly,* or you might choke.

Adverb The clown walked *sadly* away.

Adverb It is *too* quiet in here!

Adverb You seem *unusually* talkative today.

Adverb Your help was *very* appreciated.

Adverb You look *well* today.

Adverb Because he was afraid of foreigners, he treated them *xenophobically.*

Adverb She waited *yearningly* for the rain to stop.

Adverb *Zealously,* he did his homework.

Adjective The *angry* chimpanzee scolded his friend.	**Adjective** The *old* car sputtered down the road.
Adjective The North Star is the *brightest.*	**Adjective** *Pretty* peacocks fanned their tails.
Adjective The newborn baby looks so *cute*!	**Adjective** We drove through the *quaint* country village.
Adjective The *drowsy* girl fell asleep in class!	**Adjective** The *roadside* restaurant was a welcome sight to the hungry travelers.
Adjective *Early* morning is the most peaceful time of day.	**Adjective** We stayed in *six* cities during our vacation.
Adjective What a *funny* play!	**Adjective** He formed a club with his *two* new friends.
Adjective The *growing* vines wrapped around the fence.	**Adjective** What an *unusual* sight that is!
Adjective *Happy* faces were seen throughout the skating rink.	**Adjective** The kitten had *velvety* fur.
Adjective The *icy* road was dangerous for driving.	**Adjective** The *wiggly* worms wriggled in the mud.
Adjective *Jumpy* grasshoppers covered the field.	**Adjective** A *xenophobic* person is afraid of foreigners.
Adjective What a *kind* face he has!	**Adjective** The world was brightened by the rising *yellow* sun.
Adjective I feel *lazy* today.	**Adjective** The *zany* comedy team performed many wild stunts.
Adjective The *muddy* water was perfect for tadpoles.	
Adjective It was peaceful in the *natural* surroundings.	

Lesson 1B—Parts-of-Speech Bingo (*cont.*)

Parts-of-Speech Bingo

Adjective					
Adverb					
Preposition		Free			
Verb					
Noun					

Parts-of-Speech Bingo

Adjective					
Adverb					
Preposition		Free			
Verb					
Noun					

Teacher's Guide

☐ Write a list of verbs to add to the Parts of Speech page in the Writer's Notebook (page 4).

☐ As a class, do verb pantomimes. Duplicate Student Page 8 and cut apart the word cards. Have each student draw a card from a hat or basket and act out the verb for the class. The class can guess the verb. Alternatively, you can divide the students into teams and let them play as they would the game of charades. You can also have the students write or add to the list of verbs.

☐ Copy sentences from published novels and stories, leaving out the verbs. Have the students add them. They can do this as a matching exercise (with the verbs provided in a separate box), or they can use their imaginations. Afterwards, compare their choices and discuss the possibilities.

☐ Conjugate verbs. Distribute and complete Student Page 9. Also give the students page 8 from the Writer's Notebook. Here are the answers to Student Page 9:

  1. call, called, will call, have called, had called, will have called

  2. play, played, will play, have played, had played, will have played

  3. type, typed, will type, have typed, had typed, will have typed

  4. tie, tied, will tie, have tied, had tied, will have tied

  5. am, was, will be, have been, had been, will have been

  6. fly, flew, will fly, have flown, had flown, will have flown

  7. do, did, will do, have done, had done, will have done

  8. eat, ate, will eat, have eaten, had eaten, will have eaten

  9. say, said, will say, have said, had said, will have said

 10. run, ran, will run, have run, had run, will have run

☐ Determine the active or passive voice of a verb. A verb is active if the subject is doing the action of the sentence. It is passive if the subject is receiving the action or simply not doing the action. Distribute and complete Student Page 10. The answers are below. (The answers to the second section will vary.)

  1. active

  2. active

  3. passive

  4. active

  5. passive

  6. active

  7. active

  8. passive

  9. active

 10. passive

Lesson 2A—Using Verbs

bite	break	call	catch
clean	dive	drag	draw
dress	drink	eat	fall
fight	fly	freeze	frost
give	go	grow	hang
hide	kick	know	lead
lie	open	paint	pass
plant	play	plow	raise
read	ride	rise	row
run	see	send	set
shake	shine	shop	shrink
sing	sink	sit	speak
steal	swim	swing	take
tear	throw	tie	type
wake	walk	wash	wear
weave	wrap	wring	write

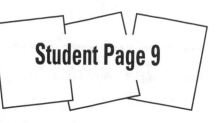

To conjugate a verb you will write it in each of its six tenses. A tense of a verb shows the time frame in which it takes place. Remember, a verb can express either action or existence.

The six tenses are as follows:

> **present tense**—happening now or regularly
> **past tense**—happened at a particular time in the past
> **future tense**—will happen
> **present perfect tense**—began in the past and continues or is completed now
> **past perfect tense**—began and was completed in the past
> **future perfect tense**—will begin and be completed in the future

Here is an example of the conjugation of a regular verb (to paint) in the first person singular (I).

> I *paint.* (present)
> I *painted.* (past)
> I *will paint.* (future)
> I *have painted.* (present perfect)
> I *had painted.* (past perfect)
> I *will have painted.* (future perfect)

Here is an example of the conjugation of an irregular verb (to draw) in the first person singular (I).

> I *draw.* (present)
> I *drew.* (past)
> I *will draw.* (future)
> I *have drawn.* (present perfect)
> I *had drawn.* (past perfect)
> I *will have drawn.* (future perfect)

Conjugate the following verbs in each of their six tenses. Use the first person singular.

1. to call _____

2. to play_____

3. to type _____

4. to tie _____

5. to be _____

6. to fly _____

7. to do _____

8. to eat_____

9. to say _____

10. to run _____

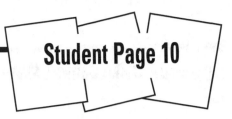

Lesson 2C—Active and Passive Verbs

Every verb has a voice. The voice shows whether the subject is doing the action of the verb (active voice) or receiving it (passive voice).

Here is an example of the active voice of the verb "to find."

I found some money in the cushion of the couch.

Here is an example of the passive voice of the verb "to find."

I was found hiding behind the tree.

After each of the sentences below, tell whether the verb is active or passive.

1. I will swim to the shore. _____
2. He sent me a letter. _____
3. The children were found after an exhaustive search. _____
4. The teacher wrote a note for the class. _____
5. She was hit by the falling hailstones. _____
6. Who sent the package to me? _____
7. They found their dog in their neighbor's yard. _____
8. The stranded people were rescued from the scene. _____
9. We walked down the street to our grandmother's house. _____
10. The baby was sent to the babysitter's house for the day. _____

Write two sentences for each of the verbs below, one in the active voice and one in the passive.

1. to hit

  a. active: _____

  _____

  b. passive: _____

  _____

2. to send

  a. active: _____

  _____

  b. passive: _____

  _____

3. to show

  a. active: _____

  _____

  b. passive: _____

  _____

Sensory words are the same regardless of what they describe. However, it is sometimes easier for students to understand them if the things described are broken down into segments. For that reason, this section of the book is divided into five parts, food, objects, animals, people, and settings.

Describing Food

☐ Prepare students to realize the importance of using sensory words to describe food. Share with them an excerpt from a book or poem they know that uses a sensory description of food. There are countless good examples.

☐ Review the list of words in the Writer's Notebook (page 9) used to describe food. Explain those words that are unfamiliar. Allow the students to add words to the list on an ongoing basis.

☐ Distribute a cookie to each student. Allow the students to experience the taste. Then, discuss attributes which apply to a description of the cookie.

☐ Distribute Student Page 11 and, as a class, write a description of the cookie.

☐ Instruct students to choose a food to describe. Then, distribute a second copy of Student Page 11 for students to complete independently. As students write the descriptive riddle on this page, encourage them to use appropriate descriptive words such as those listed on page 9 of the Writer's Notebook.

☐ Distribute Student Page 12. Ask the students to use sensory words to change each sentence. Afterwards, share and compare their responses, discussing how the sentences are improved with sensory descriptions.

☐ Ask the students to read their descriptions as the class continues to guess the food described.

☐ Begin a "Guess Who, Guess What" bulletin board on which students provide descriptive clues of something or someone, and other students try to guess what or who the description is about. For this segment, have the students provide descriptions for food. You can continue to work with the bulletin board throughout each of the following lessons on sensory words.

Additional Ideas/Notes

_____

_____

_____

_____

_____

Lesson 3A—Using Sensory Words to Describe Food

Directions: Choose a food. Using words from the Writer's Notebook (page 9) or your own ideas, fill in appropriate words. Then complete the paragraph at the bottom of the page.

Size	
Shape	
Color	
Taste	
Texture	
Odor	
Unusual Feature	

What Is It?

As large as _____ but smaller than _____, this

food is _____ in shape. Its color is _____,

and _____ is how it tastes. The texture is_____.

It smells_____. An unusual feature is _____.

What is it?_____

Directions: Rewrite each of the sentences below, using sensory words to make the sentences interesting to read. You can make each one more than one sentence.

1. The hamburger tastes good.

   _____

   _____

   _____

2. The pizza is hot.

   _____

   _____

   _____

   _____

3. I like lemonade.

   _____

   _____

   _____

   _____

4. We are having tacos for dinner.

   _____

   _____

   _____

   _____

5. Ice cream is my favorite dessert.

   _____

   _____

   _____

   _____

6. Pancakes make a good breakfast.

   _____

   _____

   _____

   _____

Teacher's Guide

Describing Objects

❑ Prepare students to realize the importance of using sensory words to describe objects. Share with them an excerpt from a book or poem they know that uses a sensory description of objects. There are countless good examples.

❑ Review the list of words in the Writer's Notebook (page 10) used to describe objects. Explain those words that are unfamiliar. Allow the students to add words to the list on an ongoing basis.

❑ Distribute a pencil or other simple object to each student. Allow the students to experience the feel and look of the pencil. Then, discuss attributes which apply to a description of the pencil.

❑ Instruct students to choose an object (other than a pencil) found in the classroom. Distribute Student Page 13 and allow students to work independently. Encourage them to use as many words as possible from the Writer's Notebook list. They may also, of course, use their own ideas. Then, ask the students to read their descriptions of the objects. While they do so, the class can endeavor to guess the objects being described.

❑ Instruct the students to use the same process as described above to describe any object (not just a classroom object). Then read their descriptions aloud while the class endeavors to guess the objects described.

❑ Distribute Student Page 14. Ask the students to use sensory words to change each sentence. Afterwards, share and compare their responses, discussing how the sentences are improved with sensory descriptions.

❑ Continue the "Guess Who, Guess What" bulletin board on which students provide descriptive clues of something or someone, and other students try to guess what or who the description is about. For this segment, have the students provide descriptions for objects. You can continue to work with the bulletin board throughout each of the following lessons on sensory words.

Additional Ideas/Notes

_____

_____

_____

_____

_____

_____

Directions: Choose an object. Using words from the Writer's Notebook (page 10) as well as your own ideas, fill in appropriate words. Then complete the paragraph at the bottom of the page.

Size/Weight	
Shape	
Color	
Texture	
Odor	
Sound	

What Is It?

The object is larger than _____ but smaller than _____. It is

_____ and _____. The texture of this object is

_____. It makes a _____ sound and has a

_____ odor. An unusual feature is _____.

What is it? _____

Lesson 3.1B—Using Sensory Sentences to Describe Objects

Directions: Rewrite each of the sentences below, using sensory words to make the sentences interesting to read. You can make each one more than one sentence.

1. The button is on my shirt.

_____

_____

_____

2. I won a trophy.

_____

_____

_____

_____

3. They played with the baseball.

_____

_____

_____

_____

4. I am going to get a hula hoop.

_____

_____

_____

5. My mother likes this bowl.

_____

_____

_____

_____

6. The car is in the garage.

_____

_____

_____

_____

Lesson 3.2—Using Sensory Words

Teacher's Guide

Describing Animals

☐ Prepare students to realize the importance of using sensory words to describe animals. Share with them an excerpt from a book or poem they know that uses a sensory description of animals. There are countless good examples.

☐ Review the list of words in the Writer's Notebook (page 11) used to describe animals and people. Explain those words that are unfamiliar. Allow the students to add words to the list on an ongoing basis.

☐ Show a picture of an animal to the class. Allow the students to study the picture. If possible, play a tape of that animal's sounds. Then, discuss attributes which apply to a description of the animal.

☐ Instruct students to choose an animal (other than the one previously chosen). Distribute Student Page 15 and allow students to work independently. Encourage them to use as many words as possible from the Writer's Notebook list. They may also, of course, use their own ideas. Then, ask the students to read their descriptions of the animals. While they do so, the class can endeavor to guess the animals being described.

☐ Distribute Student Page 16. Ask the students to use sensory words to change each sentence. Afterwards, share and compare their responses, discussing how the sentences are improved with sensory descriptions.

☐ Continue the "Guess Who, Guess What" bulletin board on which students provide descriptive clues of something or someone, and other students try to guess what or who the description is about. For this segment, have the students provide descriptions for animals. You can continue to work with the bulletin board throughout each of the following lessons on sensory words.

☐ Instruct the students to write a descriptive paragraph of an animal, using appropriate sensory words.

Additional Ideas/Notes

_____

_____

_____

_____

_____

_____

Lesson 3.2A—Using Sensory Words to Describe Animals

Directions: Choose an animal. Using words from the Writer's Notebook (page 11) as well as your own ideas, fill in appropriate words. Then complete the paragraph at the bottom of the page.

Physical Appearance	
Size	
Body Covering	
Eyes	
Ears	
Tail	
Sounds Made	
Personality	
Habitat (Home)	
Unusual Features	

What Is It?

_____ with _____ body covering, this animal has
      size

_____ eyes. It possesses _____ ears and a _____

_____ tail. With a _____, it communicates. An
                                  sound

unusual feature is_____. It is a _____ creature.
                                                         personality

This animal lives in _____.

What is it?_____

Lesson 3.2B—Using Sensory Sentences to Describe Animals

Student Page 16

Directions: Rewrite each of the sentences below, using sensory words to make the sentences interesting to read. You can make each one more than one sentence.

1. The lion is in a woodland.

____

____

____

2. I saw a peacock at the zoo.

____

____

____

____

3. This fly is annoying me.

____

____

____

____

4. My brother got a new puppy.

____

____

____

____

5. Our class has a pet tarantula.

____

____

____

____

6. A frog sat on the riverbank.

____

____

____

____

Teacher's Guide

Describing People

☐ Prepare students to realize the importance of using sensory words to describe people. Share with them an excerpt from a book or poem they know that uses a sensory description of people. There are countless good examples.

☐ Review the list of words in the Writer's Notebook (page 11) used to describe people and animals. Explain those words that are unfamiliar. Allow the students to add words to the list on an ongoing basis.

☐ Show a picture of a person to the class. Allow the students to study the picture. If possible, play an actual film or videotape of a person. Then, discuss attributes which apply to a description of the person.

☐ Instruct students to choose a person they know. Distribute Student Page 17 and allow students to work independently. Encourage them to use as many words as possible from the Writer's Notebook list. They may also, of course, use their own ideas. Then, ask the students to read their descriptions of the people. While they do so, the class can endeavor to guess the people being described. **(Note:** You may wish to restrict the group from whom they may select, such as classmates or famous people. You may also wish to advise them to make their descriptions positive and kind if they are describing real people they know. In order to avoid any hurt feelings, you can have them describe instead characters from books, stories, and movies.)

☐ Distribute Student Page 18. Ask the students to use sensory words to change each sentence. Afterwards, share and compare their responses, discussing how the sentences are improved with sensory descriptions.

☐ Continue the "Guess Who, Guess What" bulletin board on which students provide descriptive clues of something or someone, and other students try to guess what or who the description is about. For this segment, have the students provide descriptions for people. You can continue to work with the bulletin board through the following lesson on sensory words.

☐ Instruct the students to write a descriptive paragraph of a person, using appropriate sensory words.

Additional Ideas/Notes

_____

_____

_____

_____

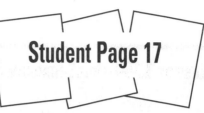
Directions: Choose a person. Using words from the Writer's Notebook (page 11) as well as your own ideas, fill in appropriate words. Then complete the paragraph at the bottom of the page.

Age	
Sex	
Stature/Body Build	
Hair	
Complexion	
Eyes	
Unusual Feature	
Personality	
Likes/Dislikes	
Talents	
Clothing	

Who Is It?

_____ with _____ hair and a _____
<small>stature</small>

complexion, _____ has _____ eyes. An unusual feature
<small>name of person</small>

is _____. He/She seems _____. _____ is
<small>personality</small>

what he/she enjoys, but he/she dislikes _____. He/She is good at

_____. This person is clothed in _____. Upon

his/her feet are _____.

Who is it? _____

Directions: Rewrite each of the sentences below, using sensory words to make the sentences interesting to read. You can make each one more than one sentence.

1. The girl is sitting at her desk.

_____

_____

_____

2. The boy is reading a book.

_____

_____

_____

_____

3. The doctor examined the broken arm.

_____

_____

_____

_____

4. The farmer plowed his fields.

_____

_____

_____

_____

5. Our teacher gave a lesson.

_____

_____

_____

_____

6. The baby giggled.

_____

_____

_____

_____

Teacher's Guide

Describing Settings

☐ Prepare students to realize the importance of using sensory words to describe settings. Share with them an excerpt from a book or poem they know that uses a sensory description of a setting. There are countless good examples.

☐ Review the list of words in the Writer's Notebook (page 12) used to describe settings. Explain those words that are unfamiliar. Allow the students to add words to the list on an ongoing basis.

☐ Show a picture of a jungle to the class. Allow the students to study the picture. If possible, play an actual film or videotape of a jungle, complete with jungle sounds. Then, discuss attributes which apply to a description of the jungle. Distribute Student Page 19 and complete it together, using the jungle as the setting.

☐ Instruct students to choose a setting other than the jungle. Distribute Student Page 19 once again and allow students to work independently. Encourage them to use as many words as possible from the Writer's Notebook list. They may also, of course, use their own ideas. Then, ask the students to read their descriptions of the settings. While they do so, the class can endeavor to guess the settings being described.

☐ Distribute Student Page 20. Ask the students to use sensory words to change each sentence. Afterwards, share and compare their responses, discussing how the sentences are improved with sensory descriptions.

☐ Complete the "Guess Who, Guess What" bulletin board on which students provide descriptive clues of something or someone, and other students try to guess what or who the description is about. For this segment, have the students provide descriptions for settings.

☐ Instruct the students to write a descriptive paragraph of a setting, using appropriate sensory words.

☐ Expand the previous descriptive paragraph into two or three paragraphs describing something that happened in the setting. In addition, people and animals can be included, also with sensory descriptions, thereby incorporating much from the previous lessons.

Additional Ideas/Notes

_____

_____

_____

_____

_____

Lesson 3.4A—Using Sensory Words to Describe Settings

Directions: Choose a setting. Using words from the Writer's Notebook (page 12) as well as your own ideas, fill in appropriate words. Then complete the paragraph at the bottom of the page.

Time	
Weather	
Plant life (if any)	
Sounds	
Sights	
Odors	
Living things (if present)	
Mood (feeling)	

Where Is It?

It is _____ in this _____ location. The weather
        _{time}   _{mood}

is _____, and one can hear _____ and

smell _____. One can also see _____

_____

_____.

Where is it? _____

Directions: Rewrite each of the sentences below, using sensory words to make the sentences interesting to read. You can make each one more than one sentence.

1. The desert is quiet.

_____

_____

_____

2. The waves hit the beach.

_____

_____

_____

3. My room is a mess.

_____

_____

_____

4. The party is wild.

_____

_____

_____

5. The valley is hot.

_____

_____

_____

6. Rain falls on the meadow.

_____

_____

_____

Lesson 4—Describing Emotions

☐ Discuss various emotions one might experience and encourage students to tell related emotional experiences.

☐ List types of emotions on the blackboard. A list is included on Student Page 21. Use it to add to the class' brainstorm, if you like. Explain any words the students do not know.

☐ Use Student Page 21 to play Emotion Charades as a class. Duplicate and cut apart the page, and allow students to draw an emotion from a hat or basket. They can each pantomime the emotion for the class or their individual teams, while the class/team guesses the emotion. (While this and the next lesson do not involve writing, they do use forms of expression that will help the students in their other writing tasks.)

☐ Also using Student Page 21, allow the students to choose an emotion from the list. Ask each student to draw a picture that corresponds to the emotion.

☐ Review and discuss words in the Writer's Notebook (page 13) that are used to express emotions. Encourage additions to the list on an ongoing basis.

☐ Distribute Student Page 22. Instruct the students to relate experiences that show the emotions. You might wish to share with them Charles M. Schulz' classic book, *Happiness Is a Warm Puppy.*

☐ Distribute Student Page 23. Instruct the students to choose three writing prompts from the list provided and to write a paragraph for each. The paragraphs can use sensory descriptions as well as imagery. Metaphors and similes will probably be useful to them. (You can teach/review metaphors and similes by turning to Lessons 11 and 12 in this book.) After the students have written their paragraphs, have them take one of them through the writing process. Display their emotions paragraphs on a bulletin board.

☐ Create a class book entitled *Emotions.* This can be comprised of the paragraphs above, poems, stories, or any other writing the class chooses to include.

Additional Ideas/Notes

_____

_____

_____

_____

_____

_____

accomplished	awkward	cocky
affectionate	bashful	comfortable
afraid	betrayed	competent
alarmed	bewildered	competitive
alert	bigger than life	confident
alive	bitter	confused
alone	bold	content
ambitious	boorish	courageous
amused	bored	cuddly
angry	brave	curious
animated	bugged	daring
annoyed	burned	defensive
anxious	calm	defiant
apprehensive	cantankerous	dejected
ashamed	cautious	depressed
assertive	claustrophobic	deserted
attractive	clever	despairing
awed	clumsy	devastated

Lesson 4A—Describing Emotions (*cont.*)

disappointed	free	impatient
disgusted	friendless	incompetent
disgraced	friendly	inspired
distracted	frightened	jealous
doubtful	frustrated	joyful
ecstatic	generous	listless
edgy	glad	lively
elated	guilty	lonely
embarrassed	happy	lovable
empathetic	harmonious	loved
empty	helpless	lovestruck
energetic	honorable	meek
engrossed	hopeful	merry
enraged	hopeless	mischievous
excited	humble	misunderstood
exhausted	humiliated	mortified
festive	hurt	nervous
frazzled	hysterical	outraged

overwhelmed	ridiculous	sociable
panicked	rushed	startled
patient	sad	surprised
patriotic	safe	suspicious
peaceful	satisfied	sympathetic
picked on	scared	terrified
playful	secure	tired
pleased	selfish	uncomfortable
powerful	sensitive	upset
powerless	serene	uptight
preoccupied	shocked	vibrant
quarrelsome	shy	vulnerable
relieved	silly	wary
repulsed	sincere	weak
resentful	small	wild
respected	smothered	wise
respectful	smug	worried

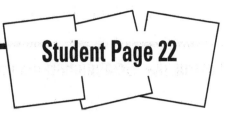

Lesson 4B—Emotion Sentences

Directions: Think of a situation which might describe each of the following emotions. Write a sentence for each. One has been done for you.

Happiness is earning an A in math.

Frustration is _____

_____

Sadness is _____

_____

Embarrassment is _____

_____

Fear is _____

_____

Love is _____

_____

Disappointment is _____

_____

Excitement is _____

_____

Curiosity is _____

_____

Contentment is _____

_____

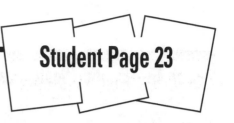

Lesson 4C—Emotion Paragraphs

Directions: Choose three different introductory sentences from the ones listed below. Expand each into a paragraph. Choose your favorite paragraph and take it through the writing process by getting a response, revising it, editing it, recopying it, and doing a final proofreading.

Include the following in your paragraph:

- When it happened
- Where it happened
- What happened
- How you felt
- Result of the experience

Cold sweat was streaming down my face.

The ocean was cold and invigorating.

The sharp sound of a rifle shot pierced the air.

The sound of thunder rumbled in the distance.

The smoke of the burning campfire filled my nose and surrounded me.

Terror struck me as I watched the horror movie.

The smell of cooking bacon called me to breakfast.

Snow fell softly from the gray sky.

I soared high above the ground in my hang glider.

Large and bold, the A appeared at the top of my math test.

My bike picked up more and more speed as it sped downhill.

Sadness filled me after the quarrel with my best friend.

Mom kissed me gently as she tucked me into bed.

Lesson 5—Using Sequential Words

There are many occasions for using sequential words. The following lessons are divided into writing how-to instructions, giving directions, and relating events.

Writing Instructions

☐ Discuss occasions for writing instructions and/or directions, particularly concerning the following:

- how to construct something
- how to prepare something
- how to do something

☐ Ask the students to brainstorm for times when such written directions must be given. Also ask them to present examples from the classroom and their textbooks.

☐ Distribute the Sequential Words page in the Writer's Notebook (page 14) and discuss when to use them. Allow the students to add words to the list on a continuing basis.

☐ Discuss a plan for writing instructions or directions. Here is one possible procedure:

- List any needed materials.
- Write directions noting correct sequential order and employing as many sequential words as possible.
- Be sure to include all important directions. Omit unnecessary directions and do not repeat instructions.
- Whenever possible, use illustrations.

☐ Distribute Student Page 24 and, as a class, write directions for how to bathe a dog. First, list the necessary materials. Next, write the directions randomly, and then number them in sequential order. Finally, tell the desired result and include an illustration.

☐ Develop with the students a list of possible things for which to write instructions. From this list, the students can choose one. Ideas for the list include how to do some of these things:

- draw a star
- fry an egg
- paint a wall
- build a model
- ride a bike
- play checkers
- make a paper boat or hat
- clean a fish tank
- make a sandwich
- build a treehouse
- rollerskate
- make a paper chain
- use a computer
- get good grades
- catch a fish
- take a message
- make a bed
- train a dog
- tie a shoelace
- peel and eat an orange
- change a tire
- clean a room
- braid hair
- write a story
- take a test
- tie a tie

☐ Instruct students to use Student Page 25 to write instructions for constructing, making, or doing anything of their choice from the brainstormed list. (If a student has an idea not on the list, allow him to do it after you have given your approval.) Urge the use of appropriate sequential words and illustrations wherever useful.

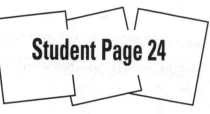

How to Bathe a Dog

Materials:

Directions:

Result:

Illustration

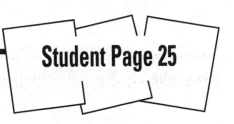
Directions: Use the form below to write instructions for constructing, making, or doing something. After writing your rough draft, take it through the writing process by getting a response, revising, editing, recopying, and doing a final proofreading.

How to

Materials/Ingredients (in a column):

Directions/Instructions (numbered):

Result:

Illustration/Diagram

Lesson 5.1—Using Sequential Words to Explain Directions

❑ Discuss the importance of giving precise directions when drawing a map or giving directions to a specific location. Have some fun by having one student provide oral directions for another blindfolded student. (Be sure that there are no safety hazards.)

❑ Discuss the appropriate sequential words on page 14 of the Writer's Notebook.

❑ Distribute Student Page 26 and, as a class, provide directions to the treasure.

❑ Emphasize to the students the important information needed to write any directions:

- Include direction words such as *east, west, north, south, right,* and *left*.
- Include appropriate sequential and number words from the Writer's Notebook.
- Name important landmarks.
- Be certain to provide directions in the correct order.
- If one is not available, draw a simple map.

❑ Present examples of places to which students may write directions:

- from home to school
- to the mall from home
- to the grocery store from home
- to the playground from the classroom
- from the classroom to the library
- from the classroom to the lunchroom
- to the theater from home
- to the shopping center from home
- from school to the nearest park

❑ Allow the students to add to the list above. Let each student choose one item from the list and write its directions, using Student Page 27. The students can share their directions and find if their classmates can determine the locations involved.

Additional Ideas/Notes

_____

_____

_____

_____

_____

Lesson 5.1A—Treasure Map

Directions: Find the treasure by following the right path. Then, write directions of exactly how to get there. Use appropriate sequential words.

Map

Directions: _____

_____

_____

_____

_____

_____

_____

_____

_____

_____

Teacher's Guide

☐ Discuss occasions for writing a sequence of events. Ideas include these:
- Writing events for a day or a week
- Writing events of a trip
- Writing an autobiography
- Writing a biography
- Writing an imaginary story about a person's life

Allow the students to brainstorm for other ideas, as well

☐ Discuss and list sequential words from the Writer's Notebook (page 14) that can be used when writing about an event. Also distribute page 15 from the Writer's Notebook on transition words. (More on transition words will be discussed in the next lesson.)

☐ Discuss a plan for writing a sequence of events. Ideas include these:
- List events to be recorded.
- Place numbers after each event to put them in correct sequential order.
- Add any omitted events.
- Delete repeated or unnecessary events.
- Illustrate one or more events.

☐ Discuss with the students how they might describe a scary night. On a large sheet of paper instruct the students to list things that happened or could happen on a scary night. List at least six but not more than 15 things. Direct the students to choose eight or fewer ideas from the list. Have them put their selected ideas on Student Page 28 in correct sequential order. Also instruct them to illustrate each event.

☐ Distribute Student Page 29 and allow the students to write a sequential autobiography. They can include a self-portrait or photographs. Perhaps you might have them bind their illustrated autobiographies inside self-made covers and display their books during a significant event, such as Open House.

☐ As an extension, allow the students to take a copy of Student Page 29 home with them to record a biography of one of their parents or family members.

Additional Ideas/Notes

_____

_____

_____

_____

Directions: Complete the following outline about an imaginary scary night. After writing a rough draft, get a response, revise, edit, recopy, and proofread.

Scary Night

This was going to be a hairy, scary night. First, at dinnertime, _____

_____

_____

(illustration)

Then at bedtime, _____

_____

_____

(illustration)

Lesson 5.2A—Using Sequential Words to Relate Events (*cont.*)

Later, at ten o'clock _____

_____

_____

(illustration)

Afterward, at midnight _____

_____

_____

(illustration)

Lesson 5.2A—Using Sequential Words to Relate Events (*cont.*)

Next, at three in the morning _____

_____

_____

(illustration)

Finally, at dawn _____

_____

_____

(illustration)

This was the hairiest, scariest night of my life!

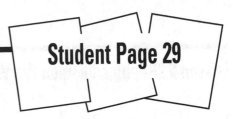

Lesson 5.2B—Using Sequential Words in an Autobiography

Directions: Complete the following autobiography, using one or more sentences about yourself for each event. After writing, go through the writing process by getting a response, revising, editing, recopying, and proofreading.

When I was born, _____

_____

_____

After I became two, _____

_____

_____

Later, when I was three, _____

_____

_____

Soon, I was five, and I _____

_____

_____

While I was in the first grade, I _____

_____

_____

When I became eight years old, I _____

_____

_____

Now I am _____, and I _____

_____

_____

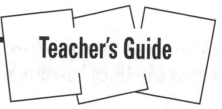

❏ When making a comparison of two things or ideas, it is often with the purpose of coming to an agreement with another person by influencing his or her opinion. Discuss this with the students.

❏ Discuss the necessity of employing transition words to demonstrate contrast between two things, to explain something, to illustrate something, to show similarities, and/or to summarize. Provide examples for the class.

❏ Using the Writer's Notebook (page 15), select some transition words that might be used when making comparisons.

❏ Distribute Student Page 30. Complete the page as a class, allowing students to become familiar with persuasive arguments.

❏ Distribute Student Page 31. Instruct the students to write a persuasive letter to their parents in support of a new bike. Have them take the letter through the writing process, incorporating as many transition words as are useful.

❏ Distribute Student Page 32 so that students might prepare a topic for persuasion on their own. Before they begin page 32, brainstorm as a class for topics from which to choose. Ideas include the following:

- baseball or football
- candy or fruit
- summer or winter
- water sports or land sports
- traditional school or year-round school
- tennis shoes or sandals
- pizza or tacos
- houses or apartments

The possible topics are endless. Be sure the students choose one about which they have something to say.

Additional Ideas/Notes

_____

_____

_____

_____

_____

_____

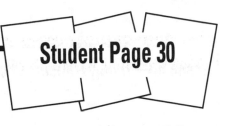

Lesson 6A—Using Transition Words

Directions: First, pretend you are trying to influence your parents to purchase a bike for you. Offer reasons and examples for each point, both for and against.

For Owning a Bike	
Reason(s)	Example(s)

Against Owning a Bike	
Reason(s)	Example(s)

Directions: Using ideas brainstormed on Student Page 30, write a letter to your parents. Use as many transition words as possible. After writing the rough draft, take your work through the writing process by getting a response, revising, editing, recopying, and proofreading.

Dear Mom and Dad,

Paragraph 1—Describe reasons for purchasing a bike. Use examples.

Paragraph 2—Describe reasons parents might give for not purchasing a bike. Counter these objections.

Paragraph 3—Summarize to prove that reasons for purchasing a bike are best.

Your loving child,

_____

(Signature)

Directions: Choose a topic that has two sides to it. Write a persuasive letter to anyone you choose, explaining why one side is better than the other. Use as many transition words as possible, making your argument flow together. Begin by brainstorming reasons and examples for or against the topic. (Use the back of this paper.) Then, write your letter below.

Topic:

Dear _____,

First paragraph—Give reasons and examples in support of the topic.

Second paragraph—Give reasons against the topic. Counter the "against" arguments.

Third paragraph—Provide a summary to prove that the "for" side is best.

Sincerely,

_____

(Signature)

Lesson 7—Using Synonyms

❑ Give the meaning of a *synonym*, a word with the same or similar meaning as another word.

❑ Discuss the value of using synonyms to accomplish more colorful, descriptive, and interesting written language.

❑ Present the list of synonyms from the Writer's Notebook (pages 16–20). Allow the students to add to the list on a continuing basis.

❑ Discuss the value of using a thesaurus to find synonyms.

❑ Distribute Student Page 33 to the class. Have them complete it in conjunction with pages 16–19 from the Writer's Notebook. They can also look in a thesaurus for other synonyms to complete the sentences.

❑ Distribute Student Page 34. The story was written by a student. Instruct the class to use Writer's Notebook pages 16–20 and/or a thesaurus to replace the italicized words with synonyms. Have the class or small groups compare their answers.

❑ After completing the above activity, duplicate some of the students' stories and have the class replace some common words with more interesting ones from pages 16–20 of the Writer's Notebook or a thesaurus.

❑ Student Page 35 contains a popular fairy tale told in basic terms. Have the students use Writer's Notebook pages 16–20 as well as a thesaurus to replace the italicized words with more descriptive ones.

Additional Ideas/Notes

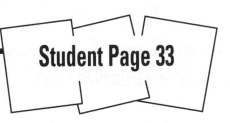

Lesson 7A—Using Synonyms

Directions: Rewrite the sentences, replacing the italicized word in each sentence with a synonym. Use the synonyms in the Writer's Notebook as a referral.

1. She did not *respond* when I called.

   _____

2. The young soldier was *brave* in the face of danger.

   _____

3. The *creek* flowed through a lovely forest.

   _____

4. The policeman could not *catch* the elusive robber.

   _____

5. I tried to *comfort* the crying baby.

   _____

6. The student did a *stupid* thing.

   _____

7. Joe is my *buddy.*

   _____

8. He will *give* me a new schedule tomorrow.

   _____

9. We read about the *bad* witch.

   _____

10. The girls can *play* in the warm sunshine.

    _____

11. The clerk asked, "May I *assist* you?"

    _____

12. The scientist discovered a new *concept* for controlling disease.

    _____

13. My father is a *big* man.

    _____

14. The young girl is extremely *lovely.*

    _____

15. My grandfather is a very *old* man.

_____

16. The athlete exhibits great *power.*

_____

17. All books must be put in their *right* order.

_____

18. The new student *shows* a lot of promise.

_____

19. You cannot *begin* until I tell you.

_____

20. The policeman *yelled,* "Halt!"

_____

21. John is a *strong* man.

_____

22. The teacher will *instruct* us in a different language.

_____

23. He is able to *tell* a story well.

_____

24. Do you *think* this school is superior in achievement?

_____

25. She was *tired* from running the long race.

_____

26. I *want* to spend more time traveling.

_____

27. I enjoy my *job.*

_____

28. When Joe came home he was *worried.*

_____

Lesson 7B—Synonym Replacement

Directions: Read the following. Replace the italicized words with synonyms from the Writer's Notebook or a thesaurus.

This is a *story* about a young boy who should listen to people instead of disregarding them.

It was the year 1997 when a *small* boy named Bob decided *to go to* the library. Bob loved to read stories about dragons and goblins. As he was *walking* to the fantasy section in the library, a *strange* book fell from the shelf. He picked it up and *thought* it was very *strange*. It *looked* as if it were hundreds of years old, and there was *weird* writing on the cover. Bob thought it was *neat,* so he looked inside, but there was no library card in it and no name on it. He took it to the librarian. She *said* he could borrow if it he returned it to the library the *next* week. He agreed.

Bob was *right:* The book was hundreds of years old. It happened that in medieval times, an *evil* wizard put a curse on it. If one read it, one would be *trapped* in a fantasy world forever. Bob was *very* excited, so much so that he ran straight home to his room and *began* to read. After he read the first word, he heard a voice say, "Beware, beware." He thought it came from the book, but he paid no attention and *kept* on reading. The book was *about* a boy just like him who also *found* a weird book. What Bob did not *know* was that the book was about him.

The next day, Bob never put the book down. When he *tried,* a force would not *let* him. So he read and read. With every page he read, he *got* more curious until he began to *think* the book was about him.

Finally, Bob was on the *last* page and he heard the voice again. "Don't read, don't read!"

Bob paid no attention and kept on reading until a *different* voice was heard and *evil* laughter arose. "You will be trapped forever fighting dragons and goblins! Ha! Ha! Ha!" *said* the evil wizard.

- Adapted from a story by Benjamin Feldman, age 10

Lesson 7C—Uncommon Fairy Tale

Directions: Read the following. Replace the italicized words with synonyms from the Writer's Notebook and a thesaurus. Use words that will make the common story much more interesting.

Jack and the Beanstalk

There once was a *boy* who lived on a *small farm* with his mother and their *cow*. They were very *poor*. A mean *giant* who lived in a *house* in the *sky* had stolen their *money*.

Jack's mother *sent* him to *town* to *sell* their cow. Instead, he *traded* it for *magic* beans. The beans *grew* into a tall beanstalk. Jack *climbed* the beanstalk into the clouds. Then he *saw* the giant's *home*.

He *asked* the giant's *wife* if he could enter. She let him in because the giant was *sleeping*. He saw a goose that laid *golden eggs, sacks* of silver and *gold,* and a golden harp. He *took* them all and *ran* to the beanstalk. The harp *said,* "Master! Master!" The giant *woke* from his *nap* and ran after Jack. He *followed* him down the beanstalk, but Jack *took* his *ax* and *chopped* down the vine. The beanstalk *fell,* and the giant *died.* Jack and his mother *lived happily* ever after.

❑ Give the definition of a *homonym,* a word that sounds the same as another word but has a different meaning.

❑ Discuss the value of using homonyms to accomplish more colorful, interesting written language.

❑ Read to the class *A Chocolate Moose for Dinner* and *Sixteen Hand Horse*, both by Fred Gwynne. These are books that give a child's eye view of several homonyms.

❑ Just as Gwynne does in his books, have the children draw an illustration to go with a homonym of their choice. Use Student Page 36.

❑ Allow the students to use their imaginations to make up homonyms. They can begin with an actual word and then change its spelling but keep the pronunciation. They must give the new word a meaning. The new words can be called *homonots.* The students can put all their homonots together in a class dictionary.

❑ Distribute Student Page 37. There are three pages that correspond to this lesson, so do as many or as few as you like. Instruct the students to complete them according to the directions. The answers are as follows:

1.	air	13.	sale	25.	hair
2.	ate	14.	so	26.	heal
3.	ball	15.	son	27.	horse
4.	bee	16.	read	28.	hole
5.	blue	17.	steal	29.	hour
6.	brake	18.	tale	30.	new
7.	by	19.	to	31.	night
8.	cent	20.	waste	32.	know
9.	deer	21.	wait	33.	made
10.	scent	22.	wear	34.	not
11.	flea	23.	week	35.	won
12.	right	24.	weather	36.	pail

❑ After completing Student Page 37, instruct the students to list the homonyms from each sentence on the worksheet in the Writer's Notebook (page 21). Allow them to add homonyms to this page on a continuing basis.

❑ Discuss homonym riddles. Here is an example:

   What happened when four couples went out to dinner? Eight ate.

❑ Encourage the students to write original homonym sentences and riddles and to use these in their written work.

Lesson 8A—Homonym Art

Directions: Choose a homonym pair and think of an illustration that shows the two of them together. For example, using the pair "eight ate," you might draw eight mice nibbling a piece of cheese. Use your imagination to help you complete this assignment.

Homonym pair: _____

Illustration

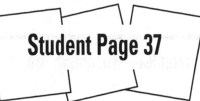

Lesson 8B—Using Homonyms

Directions: Read the sentence. On the blank, write the correct homonym for the italicized word. Then add the homonyms to page 21 of your Writer's Notebook.

1. The *heir* to the throne jogged briskly in the fresh morning _____.

2. We _____ our supper at exactly *eight* o'clock.

3. The child began to *bawl* because he could not catch the _____.

4. The beautiful bumble _____ could not *be* captured.

5. The gusty wind *blew* across the clear, _____ sky.

6. The _____ on the bike began to *break*.

7. We can *buy* delicious fruit at the stand _____ the side of the road.

8. It did not cost a _____ to purchase the new perfume *scent*.

9. A *dear* little fawn lingered near her mother _____.

10. I *sent* for the newest bubble bath _____.

11. The lively _____ jumped off the cat and began to *flee* across the room.

12. One must always use the _____ punctuation when one *writes*.

13. There was a great _____ on *sail*boats.

14. People can learn to *sew* _____ they can enjoy many different outfits.

15. The *sun* shone brightly on the king's newborn _____.

16. The police investigator _____ a note written on *red* paper.

17. Someone tried to _____ the priceless *steel* sword.

18. All the class read the _____ of Peter Cotton*tail.*

19. It was ten minutes before *two,* and we were *too* late _____ attend the movie.

20. The customer did not want to _____ her time while the saleslady took her *waist* measurement.

21. We shall not _____ for him to tell us the *weight* of the package.

22. I do not know *where* to _____ this fancy outfit.

23. The old woman felt *weak* for the entire _____.

24. The captain of the ship did not know *whether* the _____ would be satisfactory for noonday sailing.

25. The soft _____ on the baby *hare* was smooth as silk.

26. The blister on his *heel* was beginning to _____.

27. The aged gray _____ made a *hoarse* neighing sound.

28. There was a huge _____ in the ground that covered the *whole* area.

29. The _____ of *our* departure was swiftly approaching.

30. He *knew* all the _____ rock songs.

31. The brave *knight* approached the castle in the middle of the _____.

32. I _____ of *no* better way to travel than by air.

33. The efficient *maid* _____ all the beds in 30 minutes.

34. The loose *knot* could _____ hold the package together.

35. Not *one* person _____ the prize offered by the president.

36. Bending over, the *pale* maiden struggled to lift the _____ of water.

❏ Give the definition of an *antonym,* a word with the opposite meaning of another word.

❏ Discuss the value of using antonyms to accomplish more colorful, interesting written language. Encourage the use of antonyms in written work to add emphasis to ideas or thoughts.

❏ Distribute Student Page 38. Instruct the students to write a pair of antonyms at the top and to draw an illustration that shows the two and how they are opposites.

❏ Distribute Student Page 39. There are six pages that correspond to this lesson, so use as many or as few as you like. Instruct the students to complete them according to the directions. Possible answers are as follows:

1. subtract	19. front	37. hide	55. all
2. behind	20. allow	38. high	56. then
3. dead	21. bold	39. honorable	57. clear
4. none	22. ugly	40. solution	58. often
5. forbid	23. finish	41. ashamed	59. whole
6. answer	24. calm	42. correct	60. doubtful
7. together	25. adult	43. safe	61. stay
8. rests	26. opened	44. deep	62. life
9. destroyed	27. warm	45. small	63. dark
10. dishonest	28. inexpensive	46. rough	64. under
11. spacious	29. last	47. finish	65. long
12. victory	30. young	48. strong	66. loose
13. happy	31. enemy	49. take	67. abundant
14. sharp	32. poor	50. far	68. greedy
15. uneven	33. bad	51. orderly	69. halt
16. quick	34. big	52. waste	70. valuable
17. find	35. stiff	53. tranquil	71. wild
18. near	36. go	54. never	72. to

❏ After completing Student Page 39, instruct the students to list the antonyms from each sentence on the worksheet in the Writer's Notebook (page 22). Allow them to add homonyms to this page on a continuing basis.

❏ Distribute Student Page 40 and instruct the students to substitute an antonym for each italcized word in the fairy tale. Read some of their tales aloud after they have been completed. Discuss how the meaning of the tale is changed by the new words. This can be an excellent springboard for a discussion on the worth of a large vocabulary and care when choosing words to use.

❏ Use various fairy tales and change their meanings by means of an antonym substitution.

❏ Instruct the students to write original antonym sentences and to use antonyms in their written work.

❏ Encourage the use of a thesaurus when searching for antonyms.

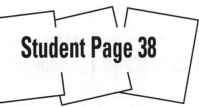
Directions: Choose an antonym pair and think of an illustration that shows how the two are opposites. For example, using the pair "over/under," you might draw one person walking over a bridge and another person swimming under it. Use your imagination to help you complete this assignment.

Antonym pair: _____

Illustration

Directions: Fill in each blank with an antonym of the italicized word in the sentence. Copy your antonym pairs in the Writer's Notebook (page 22).

1. We *add* deposits to our bank account and then _____ what we spent.

2. John was running *ahead* when Jack came up from _____.

3. My great-grandmother is *alive,* but my great-grandfather is _____.

4. You may have *all* or _____ at all.

5. I will *allow* you to watch TV, but I _____ you to stay up past 10:00 o'clock.

6. The teacher will *ask* the questions, and the students will try to_____.

7. The puzzle fell *apart,* but we put it _____.

8. The child *plays* while his mother _____.

9. The king *created* a new country after he _____ his enemies.

10. The *honest* man caught the _____ thief.

11. One room was *crowded,* and the other was _____.

12. From *defeat,* an industrious man may realize _____.

Lesson 9B—Using Antonyms (*cont.*)

13. The *downcast* woman was _____ when she found her lost jewels.

14. When he sharpened the *dull* knife, it became _____.

15. The _____ surface was sanded until it became *even.*

16. The tortoise is a *sluggish* animal, but the hare is _____.

17. I cannot _____ things I *lose.*

18. One country is *far* away, but the other is _____.

19. Joe sat in *back* of me, and Jim was in _____.

20. On this road they *ban* automobiles but _____ bicycles.

21. The princess was *bashful,* but the prince was _____.

22. The queen was *beautiful,* but the witch was _____.

23. I will *begin* my book today and _____ it tomorrow.

24. Yesterday the weather was *breezy* but today it is _____.

25. The *child* would not obey the _____.

26. The chest was *closed* until I_____ it.

27. In the north the climate is *cold,* but in the south it is _____.

28. A Mercedes is a *costly* car, but a Honda is usually _____.

29. This was the *first* part of our _____ flight.

30. The _____ boy helped the *elderly* woman across the street.

31. Tom is my *friend,* but Bill is my _____.

32. The *rich* man gave money to the _____.

33. The *good* fairy fought the _____ witch.

34. The _____ giant picked up the *little* child.

35. With heat the _____ surface became *pliable.*

36. I will let you _____ if you do not try to *stop* me.

Lesson 9B—Using Antonyms (*cont.*)

37. I tried to _____ , but they soon were able to *expose* me.

38. It was a _____ price to pay for *low* quality merchandise.

39. The _____ knight killed the *ruthless* villain.

40. He has a *problem,* and I have the _____ .

41. Mary was *proud* of her sister, but Jane was _____ of Mary.

42. The answer to problem number 9 is _____ , but the answer to problem number 10 is *inaccurate.*

43. We should make the environment _____ for *endangered* species.

44. The stream is *shallow,* but the ocean is _____ .

45. He was a _____ boy, but he had an *enormous* appetite.

46. The sand was *smooth,* but the pebble made it feel _____ .

47. We will *start* the game at 2:30 P.M. and _____ at 4:30 P.M.

48. The _____ son helped his *feeble* mother to the car.

49. I will _____ your money but *give* you food and lodging.

50. They traveled to lands *near* and _____.

51. Jim's room was _____, but Sarah's room was *disordered.*

52. We should not _____ our natural resources but *preserve* them.

53. No longer *nervous,* he became _____.

54. He _____ disobeys his parents, but *frequently* he is tempted to do so.

55. I have *nothing* in my handbag since _____ my valuables are in my luggage.

56. Don't bother me *now,* since you should have thought about that_____.

57. The *obscure* shadow now became _____.

58. I _____ fly to New York but *rarely* to Europe.

59. One quarter is *part* of the _____.

60. He was *sure* we were traveling southeast, but I was _____.

Lesson 9B—Using Antonyms (*cont.*)

61. I shall *leave,* but you may _____.

62. His _____ was abruptly ended by his quick *death.*

63. Suddenly the *light* turned to _____.

64. He swam _____ the bridge while cars drove *over* it.

65. He decided to change his _____ speech to a *brief* summary.

66. They tied the _____ rope so that it became *taut.*

67. During the famine, _____ foods became *scarce.*

68. The _____ giant took money from the *generous* prince.

69. Do not *move* when the solider says, " _____."

70. Many people made _____ donations, but the miser's gift was *worthless.*

71. The _____child hit her *mild* brother.

72. He swayed _____ and *fro* to the rhythm of the music.

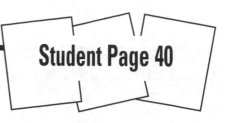

Directions: Rewrite the following story substituting corresponding antonyms for the italicized words.

Fairy Tale

Once upon a time long, long ago, there lived a *handsome prince* who was *tall* and *strong*. He possessed *beautiful, wavy* brown hair and large, *sparkling blue* eyes. He wore the *finest* apparel of *silk* and *satin* and carried a silver *sword* which he used to perform *good* deeds of *courage* and *bravery*. This prince was a *happy* man because everyone in the kingdom *loved* and *respected* him. He was *popular* and had many *friends*. One day he married a *lovely princess*, and they lived a *long* and *joyful* life.

☐ Give the definition of a *simile,* a phrase that compares two unlike things in order to describe one of them. Similes use the word *like* or *as* in order to make the comparison.

☐ Read *Quick as a Cricket* by Don and Audrey Wood to the class.

☐ Discuss the value of using similes to accomplish more colorful, interesting written language. Encourage the use of similes in written work to add emphasis to ideas or thoughts.

☐ Distribute Student Page 41 (there are two sheets). Instruct the students to choose a simile from the provided list. Then ask the students to draw an illustration that shows the meaning of their chosen simile, similar to what is done in *Quick as a Cricket.* The second sheet can also be used for students to illustrate similes that they write themselves. The pages can then be collected and displayed or turned into a class simile book.

☐ Distribute Student Page 42. Instruct the students to complete the similes. They can then add their original similes to the Writer's Notebook, page 23. Students can also add to this page on a continuing basis.

☐ Distribute Student Page 43. Instruct the students to complete the sentences, using similes.

☐ Distribute Student Page 44. Instruct the students to write a brief simile poem for each of the provided beginnings as well as for one idea of their own.

Additional Ideas/Notes

_____

_____

_____

_____

_____

_____

_____

_____

_____

_____

Directions: Choose a simile from the list below. Remember, a simile is a word picture comparison of two unlike things, using *like* or *as.* Once you have made your choice, write it on the next page.

blind as a bat
brave as a lion
cheap as dirt
clean as a whistle
cold as ice
crazy as a loon
deaf as a post
dumb as an ox
easy as pie
fat as a hog
fit as a fiddle
flat as a flounder
gentle as a lamb
good as gold
green as grass
hard as nails
light as a feather
mad as a hatter
neat as a pin
nervous as a cat
playful as a kitten
pleased as punch
pretty as a picture
proud as a peacock
quick as a wink
right as rain
sharp as a tack
shy as a violet
sick as a dog
sly as a fox
smart as a whip
stubborn as a mule
straight as an arrow
strong as an ox
sweet as sugar
thin as a rail
warm as toast
white as a sheet
wrinkled as a prune

Lesson 10A—Similes as Word Pictures (*cont.*)

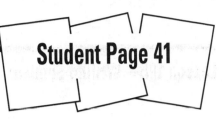

Directions: Choose a simile from the previous page and write it below. Then draw an illustration that shows the simile. Use your imagination to help you complete this assignment.

Simile: _____

Illustration

Directions: Complete the following similes and add them to the Writer's Notebook (page 23).

lively as _____

swift as _____

slow as _____

funny as _____

red as _____

soft as _____

tiny like _____

soft as _____

happy like _____

fierce as _____

quiet like _____

slippery as _____

bright as _____

graceful as _____

wiggly as _____

quiet as _____

shaggy as _____

shy as _____

ugly as _____

bright as _____

loud as _____

huge as _____

thick as _____

brave as _____

tiny as _____

clumsy as _____

gentle as _____

grumpy as _____

hard as _____

playful as _____

fuzzy as _____

mischievous as _____

proud as _____

peaceful as _____

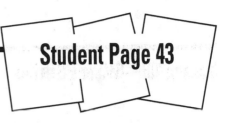

Lesson 10C—Using Similes

Directions: Complete each of the following sentences with a simile. For each one, try to paint a word picture.

Example: The girl frolicking in the water looked like a playful dolphin jumping through the clear, blue ocean.

1. The school library was as quiet as _____.

2. The young Olympic runner sprinting down the path was as swift as_____.

3. The small child playing in the garden was as playful as _____.

4. The pretty young girl dancing on the stage was as happy as _____.

5. The icy, city sidewalk was as slippery as _____.

6. Snuggling under the warm comforter, the child felt as cozy as_____.

7. Showing his report card to his parents, the boy was as proud as _____.

8. After the snowfall, the ground looked like _____.

9. Under the cover of darkness, the animals of the forest gathered like_____.

10. The boisterous crowd cheered their team like _____.

11. Hearing the shrill whistle of the train was like _____.

12. At midnight, the tardy teenager crept into the house like _____.

Directions: Complete each simile below to write a brief poem. (It does not have to rhyme, but it should be written in lines of verse.) Then write a complete simile poem of your own on the back of this page.

Example: Winter is as tempestuous . . .

Winter is as tempestuous as the ocean waves crashing onto shore during a storm.

Example: A baby is as cuddly . . .

A baby is as cuddly as a soft, furry kitten lounging on your lap.

Write a simile poem for the following or make up your own comparison.

A tiger is as fierce as

_____

_____

A bird is as free as

_____

_____

Summer is as joyful as

_____

_____

Lesson 11—Using Metaphors

☐ Give the definition of a *metaphor,* a phrase that compares two unlike things. Discuss the differences between a simile and a metaphor. A simile compares two things that are not alike by using the words *as* or *like.* A metaphor, although it also compares two unlike things, says that one thing *is* the other.

☐ Discuss the value of using metaphors to accomplish more colorful, interesting written language. Encourage the use of metaphors in written work to add emphasis to ideas or thoughts.

☐ Distribute Student Page 45 (two sheets). Instruct the students to complete each metaphor. They can add their metaphors to page 24 of the Writer's Notebook. Have the class share their different ideas with one another so that any metaphors the students hear and like, they can copy into their own Writer's Notebook page.

☐ Review the metaphors in the Writer's Notebook (page 24) and, as a class, think of other metaphors to add to the page.

☐ Distribute Student Page 46 (two sheets). Instruct the students to write a brief metaphoric poem for each of the provided beginnings as well as for one idea of their own. Then ask the students to choose one poem, recopy it onto the second sheet, and draw an illustration that shows the poem's meaning. The poems and illustrations can be displayed or collected into a class book.

Additional Ideas/Notes

_____

_____

_____

_____

_____

_____

_____

_____

_____

_____

_____

Directions: Complete each phrase below by writing a metaphor. Remember, a metaphor compares two things that are not alike but says that one thing is the other. Add your completed metaphors to the Writer's Notebook (page 24). Also add any of your classmates' metaphors that you like.

The rain is _____

_____

An abandoned town is _____

_____

The new car is _____

_____

The earth is _____

_____

The Golden Gate Bridge is _____

_____

The carnival is _____

_____

A tree is _____

_____

The barbecue is _____

_____

Comic books are _____

_____

Television is _____

_____

My family is _____

_____

Music is _____

_____

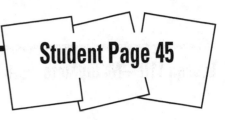

Lesson 11A—Using Metaphors (*cont.*)

Dancing is_____

_____

Baseball is _____

_____

The Olympics are _____

_____

Blue jeans are _____

_____

Chocolate cake is _____

_____

Frogs are_____

_____

The zoo is _____

_____

Pancakes for breakfast are_____

_____

Receiving an A is _____

_____

Race cars are_____

_____

Time is_____

_____

Puppies are _____

_____

Directions: Metaphoric poetry employs an interesting way to show something by comparing it to another, unrelated thing.

Examples:

Winter is a chill
To waken your senses.

Home is a heavenly haven
Of love, warmth, and security.

Make the following metaphors into poetry. (It does not have to rhyme.) Finally, write a complete metaphor poem of your own.

School is_____

_____

_____

_____

Mom (Dad) is_____

_____

_____

_____

Friendship is _____

_____

_____

_____

My own: _____

_____

_____

_____

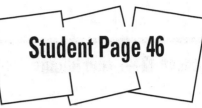

Lesson 11B—Metaphoric Poetry (*cont.*)

Directions: Choose one of your poems from the previous page and write it on the lines below. Draw an illustration that shows the poem's meaning.

Poem:_____

_____

_____

_____

Illustration

Lesson 12—Using Idioms

❑ Give the definition of an *idiom,* a group of words whose meaning differs from the actual words being used. For example, to say, "The son gave his dad a lot of double-talk," literally means, "The son did not tell his dad the way things really were."

❑ Discuss the value of using idioms to accomplish more colorful, interesting written language. Encourage the appropriate use of idioms in written work to add emphasis to ideas or thoughts.

❑ Ask the students to share idioms with which they are familiar.

❑ Distribute Student Page 47 (two sheets). Instruct the students to match each idiom to its meaning. Here are the correct answers:

1. n	11. gg	21. aa	31. kk
2. k	12. j	22. h	32. ii
3. t	13. l	23. r	33. jj
4. p	14. c	24. x	34. dd
5. d	15. ee	25. o	35. u
6. a	16. e	26. cc	36. ff
7. i	17. s	27. m	37. nn
8. g	18. bb	28. z	38. hh
9. f	19. y	29. v	39. w
10. q	20. ll	30. mm	40. b

Have the students add these idioms to page 25 of the Writer's Notebook.

❑ Review the idioms in the Writer's Notebook (page 25) and, as a class, think of other idioms to add to the page.

❑ Distribute Student Page 48 (two sheets). Instruct the students to write sentences that incorporate each of the idioms listed.

Additional Ideas/Notes

_____

_____

_____

_____

_____

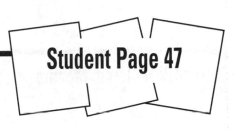

Lesson 12A—Idiom Meanings

Directions: Keeping in mind that idioms are groups of words where meaning differs from the actual words, match the Idiom Column to Meaning Column. Copy and add to Writer's Notebook.

Idiom Column

1. born with a silver spoon in his mouth
2. neat as a pin
3. put the cart before the horse
4. walking on air
5. kill two birds with one stone
6. leave no stone unturned
7. through thick and thin
8. hold your horses
9. spill the beans
10. eat one's heart out
11. blow off steam
12. keep a stiff upper lip
13. hit the ceiling
14. pay off
15. pain in the neck
16. shaking in your boots
17. easy as falling off a log
18. lend me a hand
19. cry over spilt milk
20. put your foot in your mouth

Meaning Column

a. to be very thorough
b. a mix of sense and nonsense language
c. reward
d. to accomplish two things at once
e. frightened
f. tell a secret
g. wait patiently
h. to be hoarse
i. to stand by in good times and in bad
j. to be brave
k. extremely tidy
l. become very angry
m. agree
n. to have everything you want
o. be quiet
p. extremely happy
q. to be jealous
r. passing time in meaningless ways while waiting
s. simple to do
t. to do something backwards

Idiom Column

21. blew it

22. frog in her throat

23. kill some time

24. getting in my hair

25. hold your tongue

26. raining cats and dogs

27. see eye to eye

28. in the doghouse

29. fork in the road

30. mountain of work

31. cut up

32. hold up

33. talking through your hat

34. fit as a fiddle

35. driving me up the wall

36. turn over a new leaf

37. monkey on your back

38. live down

39. downhearted

40. double-talk

Meaning Column

u. making me feel crazy

v. division in the road

w. saddened

x. bothering me

y. worry about what you cannot change

z. in trouble

aa. failed

bb. help me

cc. raining hard

dd. in good condition

ee. annoying

ff. begin again

gg. saying or doing things angrily to relieve pressure

hh. wipe out of memory

ii. robbery

jj. talking foolishness

kk. act like a comic

ll. say what I should not say

mm. a lot to do

nn. annoying circumstance, person, or habit

Lesson 12B—Using Idioms

Directions: Write sentences for the following idioms.

1. walking on air_____

   _____

2. pay off _____

   _____

3. put my foot in my mouth _____

   _____

4. raining cats and dogs_____

   _____

5. in the doghouse_____

   _____

6. fork in the road _____

   _____

7. hit the ceiling _____

   _____

8. blow off steam_____

   _____

9. keep a stiff upper lip_____

   _____

10. hold up_____

   _____

Lesson 12B—Using Idioms (*cont.*)

11. born with a silver spoon in your mouth _____

_____

12. neat as a pin _____

_____

13. put the cart before the horse _____

_____

14. kill two birds with one stone _____

_____

15. leave no stone unturned _____

_____

16. through thick and thin _____

_____

17. hold your horses _____

_____

18. spill the beans _____

_____

19. eat one's heart out _____

_____

20. easy as falling off a log _____

_____

☐ Discuss the meaning of *alliteration,* the repetition of the beginning sound of two or more words in a sentence to emphasize a description or point.

Examples:

The shining sun shone on the silent seashore.

Duke, the diligent dog, dug a deep hole.

☐ Assign Student Page 49 (two sheets) in which students will write alliterative phrases or sentences for each of the phrases provided. One such alliterative sentence will be expanded into a one- or two-paragraph story with a corresponding illustration.

☐ Instruct the students to copy their alliterative sentences onto page 26 of the Writer's Notebook. Ask them to share their ideas with one another so that students can also copy down the alliterative sentences of their peers. Have them add to this page on an ongoing basis.

☐ Instruct each student to choose an alliterative story title from pages 89–95. (Reproduce the pages and cut out each story title. Students can attach the titles to a cover sheet, page 96, for their stories.) Students then write short stories about their chosen titles, using some alliteration. Display the completed stories on a wall or large bulletin board entitled "An Alphabet of Alliterative Stories."

Arial, the Acrobatic Arachnid

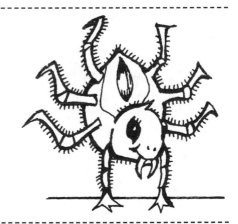

Buddy, the Busy Beaver

Clara, the Courteous Cow

Devouring a Divine Dessert

Ethel, the Elegant Elephant

The Fabulous Fudge Factory

Giselle, the Graceful Gazelle

Home for a Happy Hippo

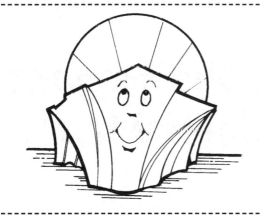

Iggy, Iceland's Incredible Iceberg

The Jumping Jackrabbit Joust

Kicking Kangaroo Congregation

Lola's Luscious Lollipop Luau

Monty's Marvelous Milkshake Manor

Nine Nifty Neckties

Oscar, the Odd Octopus

Perky Pets on Parade

Quick Quail Quandary

Reginald, the Refined Rat

Slippery Sue, the Sleek Seal

Tovah's Tasty Treats

Eunice's Unique Umbrella

The Villainous, Venomous Viper

Wanda the Wiggly Worm

Xavier's Excellent Xylophone

Yogi, the Yummy Yam

Zealous Zebras and the Zany Zoo

(Paste title here.)

_____

_____

_____

_____

_____

_____

_____

_____

_____

_____

_____

_____

_____

_____

_____

_____

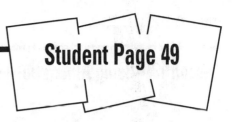

Lesson 13—Using Alliteration

Directions: *Alliteration* is the repetition of a sound at the beginning of several words together in a sentence to emphasize a description or a certain point. Use alliteration to describe each of the following people, objects, or things. Then choose one of your alliterative sentences and expand it into a short one- or two-paragraph story. After writing the rough draft, revise, edit, recopy, and proofread it, using the next page. You will also add an illustration.

Add all your examples of alliteration to the Writer's Notebook (page 26).

1. a silly girl _____

_____

2. a super singing star _____

_____

3. a household pet _____

_____

4. Santa Claus _____

_____

5. Halloween night _____

_____

6. sailing at sunset _____

_____

7. a cat _____

_____

8. a bird flying _____

_____

9. a clown _____

_____

10. a dinosaur _____

_____

11. a country fair _____

_____

12. a circus _____

_____

13. a horse _____

_____

Alliterative sentence: _____

_____

Story: _____

_____

_____

_____

_____

_____

_____

_____

_____

_____

_____

Illustration

☐ Give the definition of *hyperbole,* an exaggerated statement. Hyperbole is somewhat like a metaphor in that one thing is said to be something else that is not realistic.

> **Example:** It was so hot I was burning up.

☐ Discuss the examples of hyperbole provided on page 27 of the Writer's Notebook. Allow the students to add their own examples to the page on a continuing basis.

☐ Discuss the value of using hyperbole to create more colorful, interesting written language. Encourage the use of hyperbole in written work where it will add emphasis to ideas or thoughts.

☐ Distribute Student Page 50 (two sheets) and instruct the students to rewrite each statement as a hyperbole. Allow them to share their ideas and to add them to page 27 of the Writer's Notebook.

☐ Distribute Student Page 51. Tell the students the meaning of a "fish story," an exaggerated tale that is derived from fishermen's tendencies to exaggerate the size of the fish they catch when telling other people of their adventures. Have the students tell fish stories of their own, using the provided page. They can use page 27 of the Writer's Notebook for ideas. Display the students' fish stories on a bulletin board or in a class book. For a bulletin board display, create a fishing pole from construction paper, add string for fishing line, and place the fish along the line. Entitle the board "Fish Stories" or "The Ones That Nearly Got Away."

Additional Ideas/Notes

_____

_____

_____

_____

_____

_____

_____

_____

_____

Directions: Rewrite each of the following statements as *hyperbole,* an exaggerated statement written for emphasis.

1. The snow was cold. _____

_____

2. I felt happy. _____

_____

3. The car was fast. _____

_____

4. The concert was loud. _____

_____

5. The amusement park is fun. _____

_____

6. The beach was crowded. _____

_____

7. I am an excellent athlete. _____

_____

8. I did well on my test. _____

_____

9. My father is tall. _____

_____

10. The house was painted bright yellow. _____

_____

11. The class was busy. _____

_____

12. The day was hot. _____

_____

13. The book is long. _____

_____

14. Her hair was long. _____

_____

15. The dog is small. _____

_____

16. The bear was large. _____

_____

17. The workers were loud. _____

_____

18. He was a good person. _____

_____

19. The show is boring. _____

_____

20. I am late. _____

_____

Lesson 14B—Fish Story

Directions: A "fish story" is an exaggerated tale that is derived from fishermen's tendencies to exaggerate the size of the fish they catch when telling other people of their adventures. A fish story can be about anything; it simply must be exaggerated. Tell a fish story of your own, using the space below to write your final copy.

Lesson 15—Using Personification

☐ Give the meaning of *personification*, the technique of assigning animate qualities to inanimate things. Also discuss the value of using personification as a writing device that adds interest and meaning.

☐ Discuss the examples of personification provided in the Writer's Notebook (page 28).

☐ Assign Student Page 52 and instruct the students to find something animate about each of the items listed. For example, a picture might "look back" at someone. Add these examples of personification to the Writer's Notebook (page 28).

☐ Student Pages 53 (four sheets) include four writing prompts, each involving personification. Instruct the students to select one of the four and to take it through the writing process, copying the final draft onto the provided sheet. Share their stories in small groups or whole class, and then display them together in a class book.

☐ Student Page 54 involves reverse personification, taking an animate object and removing its ability to move and function. Have the students write a story about themselves as if they suddenly became inanimate, perhaps by turning to stone. They should use the writing process in order to finalize their stories. Share the stories in small groups or whole class. Collect them and display them with the stories from Student Page 53.

Additional Ideas/Notes

Directions: *Personification* is the technique of assigning animate qualities to inanimate things. Think of something human about each of the following objects and write a sentence about it, using personification.

What can a picture do?_____

_____

What can a pencil do?_____

_____

What can a car do? _____

_____

What can a bush do?_____

_____

What can dewdrops do? _____

_____

What can a lamp do? _____

_____

What can a cloud do? _____

_____

What can a river do? _____

_____

What can a pebble do? _____

_____

Directions: Write a story, beginning with the prompt below. Use personification, the technique of giving animation to inanimate things, as the basis for your story.

Prompt: The Day I Became a Pencil

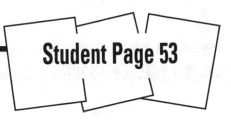

_____

_____

_____

_____

_____

_____

_____

_____

_____

_____

_____

_____

_____

_____

_____

Directions: Write a story, beginning with the prompt below. Use personification, the technique of giving animation to inanimate things, as the basis for your story.

Prompt: My Life as the Family Car

_____

_____

_____

_____

_____

_____

_____

_____

_____

_____

_____

_____

_____

_____

_____

_____

_____

_____

_____

_____

Lesson 15B—Personification Stories *(cont.)*

Directions: Write a story, beginning with the prompt below. Use personification, the technique of giving animation to inanimate things, as the basis for your story.

Prompt: Just Call on Me, the Telephone

_____

_____

_____

_____

_____

_____

_____

_____

_____

_____

_____

_____

_____

_____

_____

_____

_____

_____

Directions: Write a story, beginning with the prompt below. Use personification, the technique of giving animation to inanimate things, as the basis for your story.

Prompt: I May Be a Computer, but I Don't Byte

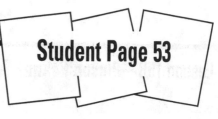

_____

_____

_____

_____

_____

_____

_____

_____

_____

_____

_____

_____

_____

_____

_____

_____

_____

_____

_____

_____

Lesson 15B—Reverse Personification Stories

Directions: Imagine you are walking along one day, and suddenly you become a completely inanimate object. What happened? Do you still have the ability to think? What becomes of you? Write an imaginary story about your experiences. Use the writing process and write your final draft below.

_____

_____

_____

_____

_____

_____

_____

_____

_____

_____

_____

_____

_____

_____

_____

_____

_____

_____

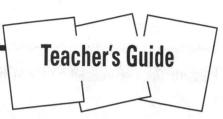

❏ Encourage students to become aware of unusual descriptive word combinations in literature. These descriptions are similar to metaphors in that unlike things are often compared in order to create emphasis. They are also sometimes oxymoronic in effect, combining two things that should be mutually exclusive. Regardless of the form they take, the result of the word combinations is an unusual description that captures the reader's attention and imagination, painting a vivid picture for the reader to envision.

❏ Discuss the value of using such descriptions as a writing device that adds interest, variety, and enhanced meaning to written language.

❏ As an ongoing process, have the students add such descriptions to the Writer's Notebook (page 29).

❏ Distribute Student Page 55 (two sheets) and instruct the students to draw pictures to illustrate the phrases. They can then copy the phrases into the Writer's Notebook (page 29).

❏ Instruct students to choose a descriptive sentence from Student Page 55 and to expand it into a descriptive paragraph.

❏ Distribute Student Page 56. Have the students complete each sentence with a description that involves an unusual word combination. Encourage them to think of their previous work with metaphors, similes, and other imagistic language. You might wish to review those lessons before they begin this exercise.

❏ Distribute Student Page 57 (two sheets). Instruct the students to write a descriptive sentence (in the manner of the sentences in the Writer's Notebook, page 29) for each of the pictures provided.

❏ Instruct students to choose a descriptive sentence from Student Page 57 and to expand it into a descriptive paragraph.

❏ Add the sentences from Student Page 57 to the Writer's Notebook (page 29).

Additional Ideas/Notes

_____

_____

_____

_____

_____

_____

Directions: Draw a picture to illustrate each descriptive sentence. Write each sentence in the Writer's Notebook (page 29).

The raging storm at sea brightened the tropical island.

The first rays of sunlight cast long shadows over the landscape.

Bright yellow daffodils carpeted a distant field.

A mighty eagle called and soared above the still, quiet desert.

The desolate shack broke the monotony of the vast plains.

Cornstalks stood alone like silent soldiers in the autumn field.

Lesson 16B—Writing Unusual Word Combinations

Directions: Write a sentence for each phrase that employs a description involving an unusual word combination. One has been done for you. Add your descriptions to page 29 of the Writer's Notebook.

Example: a fire-burned landscape

Sentence: The small, white rabbits dotted the sooty, fire-burned landscape like cottonballs as they came out to explore the fire's aftermath.

1. scampering kittens _____

   _____

2. sleeping children _____

   _____

3. a wailing baby _____

   _____

4. a noisy crowd _____

   _____

5. a schoolyard fight _____

   _____

6. a smoke-filled room _____

   _____

7. a flower-decorated hat _____

   _____

8. chattering monkeys in the trees _____

   _____

9. three lazy bears _____

   _____

10. a dripping strawberry Popsicle _____

   _____

Directions: Write a sentence that uses an unusual word combination to describe each of the pictures below. Add your sentences to page 29 of the Writer's Notebook.

Sentence:

Sentence:

Sentence:

Lesson 16C—Writing Unusual Word
        Combinations from Images (*cont.*)

Sentence:

Sentence:

Sentence:

Lesson 17— How to Expand Sentences

☐ Review the components of a complete sentence: a subject and a predicate, expressing a complete thought.

☐ Read to the class the following two sentences.

- The car went down the street.
- The fiery red, streamlined Corvette skidded crazily down the rain-drenched street like a runaway freight car and nearly struck the lazy, lumbering, little dog who was crossing the street.

☐ Discuss how the sentences differ. Write the two sentences on the board and take them apart, diagramming the various components.

☐ As a class, expand the following sentence.

The lion roared.

1. Add two descriptive words (adjectives).

   The **mighty**, **angry** lion roared.

2. Add how (adverb or adverbial phrase).

   The mighty, angry lion roared **loudly**.

3. Add where (prepositional phrase).

   The mighty, angry lion, roared loudly **in the jungle**.

4. Add when (prepositional phrase).

   The mighty, angry lion roared loudly in the jungle **at nightfall**.

5. Add why.

   The mighty, angry lion roared loudly in the jungle at nightfall **because he could not find his mate**.

6. Use a simile or metaphor.

   The mighty, angry lion roared **as loud as thunder** in the jungle at nightfall . . . .

7. Use alliteration.

   The large, lazy lion loudly roared in the jungle at nightfall because . . . .

8. Use personification.

   The large, lazy lion loudly roared in the **screaming jungle** at nightfall because . . . .

9. Use hyperbole.

   The large, lazy lion roared so loudly that **he shook the trees in the jungle** . . . .

☐ Discuss the pattern for sentence expansion followed above. Distribute page 30 in the Writer's Notebook.

☐ Distribute Student Page 58 (six sheets). Instruct the students to follow the sentence expansion pattern for each of them (or as many as you choose). Afterwards, have the students share their ideas.

☐ Instruct the students to expand other simple sentences in ways of their choice. Use Student Page 59.

Lesson 17A— How to Expand Sentences

Directions: Follow the pattern to expand and alter each sentence. Use page 30 of the Writer's Notebook for help.

The teacher screamed.

1. Add two adjectives. _____

   _____

   _____

2. Add how (adverb). _____

   _____

   _____

3. Add where (prepositional phrase). _____

   _____

   _____

4. Add when (prepositional phrase). _____

   _____

   _____

5. Add why. _____

   _____

   _____

6. Use a simile or metaphor, if possible. _____

   _____

   _____

7. Use alliteration, if possible. _____

   _____

   _____

8. Use personification, if possible. _____

   _____

   _____

9. Use hyperbole, if possible. _____

   _____

10. Use as many synonyms as possible for the given words. _____

    _____

The snake hissed.

1. Add two adjectives. _____

_____

_____

2. Add how (adverb). _____

_____

_____

3. Add where (prepositional phrase). _____

_____

_____

4. Add when (prepositional phrase). _____

_____

_____

5. Add why. _____

_____

_____

6. Use a simile or metaphor, if possible. _____

_____

_____

7. Use alliteration, if possible. _____

_____

_____

8. Use personification, if possible. _____

_____

_____

9. Use hyperbole, if possible. _____

_____

_____

10. Use as many synonyms as possible for the given words. _____

_____

_____

The child wept.

1. Add two adjectives. _____

_____

_____

2. Add how (adverb). _____

_____

_____

3. Add where (prepositional phrase). _____

_____

_____

4. Add when (prepositional phrase). _____

_____

_____

5. Add why. _____

_____

_____

6. Use a simile or metaphor, if possible. _____

_____

_____

7. Use alliteration, if possible. _____

_____

_____

8. Use personification, if possible. _____

_____

_____

9. Use hyperbole, if possible. _____

_____

_____

10. Use as many synonyms as possible for the given words. _____

_____

_____

Lesson 17A— How to Expand Sentences (*cont.*)

The policeman ran.

1. Add two adjectives. _____
_____
_____

2. Add how (adverb). _____
_____
_____

3. Add where (prepositional phrase). _____
_____
_____

4. Add when (prepositional phrase). _____
_____
_____

5. Add why. _____
_____
_____

6. Use a simile or metaphor, if possible. _____
_____
_____

7. Use alliteration, if possible. _____
_____
_____

8. Use personification, if possible. _____
_____
_____

9. Use hyperbole, if possible. _____
_____
_____

10. Use as many synonyms as possible for the given words. _____
_____
_____

The ship sailed.

1. Add two adjectives. _____

_____

_____

2. Add how (adverb). _____

_____

_____

3. Add where (prepositional phrase). _____

_____

_____

4. Add when (prepositional phrase). _____

_____

_____

5. Add why. _____

_____

_____

6. Use a simile or metaphor, if possible. _____

_____

_____

7. Use alliteration, if possible. _____

_____

_____

_____

8. Use personification, if possible. _____

_____

_____

9. Use hyperbole, if possible. _____

_____

_____

10. Use as many synonyms as possible for the given words. _____

_____

_____

The dog howled.

1. Add two adjectives. _____

_____

_____

2. Add how (adverb). _____

_____

_____

3. Add where (prepositional phrase). _____

_____

_____

4. Add when (prepositional phrase). _____

_____

_____

5. Add why. _____

_____

_____

6. Use a simile or metaphor, if possible. _____

_____

_____

7. Use alliteration, if possible. _____

_____

_____

8. Use personification, if possible. _____

_____

_____

9. Use hyperbole, if possible. _____

_____

_____

10. Use as many synonyms as possible for the given words. _____

_____

_____

Lesson 17B—Sentences to Expand

Directions: Choose 10 of the following sentences and expand them in any way you like to make them as interesting and detailed as you can.

a. I laughed.	k. Bikes raced.
b. We skipped.	l. The river runs.
c. The boat sails.	m. You sang.
d. Rain is falling.	n. The vines climb.
e. The grass grew.	o. Children played.
f. People danced.	p. Trains moved.
g. The runner leaped.	q. The chick hatched.
h. The doctor smiled.	r. The fans yell.
i. The waves break.	s. Flowers bloom.
j. My father hiked.	t. Presents were wrapped.

1. _____
   _____

2. _____
   _____

3. _____
   _____

4. _____
   _____

5. _____
   _____

6. _____
   _____

7. _____
   _____

8. _____
   _____

9. _____
   _____

10. _____
    _____

Lesson 18—Ways to Begin a Sentence

☐ Discuss the importance of using different sentence beginnings to give one's writing a sense of variety. Similar beginnings make reading monotonous and can lose the reader's interest.

☐ Discuss Ways to Begin a Sentence (page 31) and Sentence Starters (page 32) in the Writer's Notebook.

☐ There are many ways to begin a sentence. Page 31 in the Writer's Notebook outlines some of them. Using page 31 as a guideline, work as a class through the following example of alternative sentence beginnings.

> **Sentence:** Firemen fight fires.
>
> **Adjectives:** Strong, brave firemen fight fires.
>
> > or
> >
> > Strong and brave firemen fight fires.
>
> **Question:** How do firemen fight fires?
>
> **Prepositional phrase:** At the blazing building, firemen fight the fire.
>
> **Infinitive Verb ("to" plus verb):** To put out the blazing building, firemen use great quantities of water.
>
> **Gerund Verb (verb plus "ing"):** Fighting the fire with all their might, the firemen finally conquer the blaze.
>
> **Interjection:** Wow! What a heroic job the firemen performed.

☐ Distribute Student Page 60 (six sheets). Instruct the students to alternate the beginning of each sentence according to the directions and the guidelines on page 31 of the Writer's Notebook. (You can distribute as many or as few of the six sheets as you like.)

☐ Have the students add other useful words for the beginnings of sentences to the ones provided on Writer's Notebook page 32.

● Additional Ideas/Notes ●

_____

_____

_____

_____

_____

Directions: Rewrite the sentence below, following the instruction provided. Use page 31 from the Writer's Notebook to help you.

Lions fight.

1. Begin with two adjectives. _____

_____

_____

2. Begin with a question. _____

_____

_____

3. Begin with a prepositional phrase. _____

_____

_____

4. Begin with an infinitive verb. _____

_____

_____

5. Begin with a gerund verb. _____

_____

_____

6. Begin with an interjection. _____

_____

_____

Lesson 18A—Ways to Begin a Sentence (*cont.*)

Directions: Rewrite the sentence below, following the instruction provided. Use page 31 from the Writer's Notebook to help you.

Boys run.

1. Begin with two adjectives. _____

_____

_____

2. Begin with a question. _____

_____

_____

3. Begin with a prepositional phrase. _____

_____

_____

4. Begin with an infinitive verb. _____

_____

_____

_____

5. Begin with a gerund verb. _____

_____

_____

6. Begin with an interjection. _____

_____

_____

Directions: Rewrite the sentence below, following the instruction provided. Use page 31 from the Writer's Notebook to help you.

Soldiers fight.

1. Begin with two adjectives. _____

_____

_____

2. Begin with a question. _____

_____

_____

3. Begin with a prepositional phrase. _____

_____

_____

4. Begin with an infinitive verb. _____

_____

_____

5. Begin with a gerund verb. _____

_____

_____

6. Begin with an interjection. _____

_____

_____

Directions: Rewrite the sentence below, following the instruction provided. Use page 31 from the Writer's Notebook to help you.

Chimps chatter.

1. Begin with two adjectives. _____

_____

_____

2. Begin with a question. _____

_____

_____

3. Begin with a prepositional phrase. _____

_____

_____

4. Begin with an infinitive verb. _____

_____

_____

5. Begin with a gerund verb. _____

_____

_____

6. Begin with an interjection. _____

_____

_____

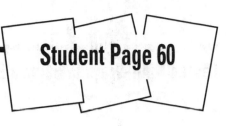

Directions: Rewrite the sentence below, following the instruction provided. Use page 31 from the Writer's Notebook to help you.

The swimmer dove.

1. Begin with two adjectives. _____

_____

_____

2. Begin with a question. _____

_____

_____

3. Begin with a prepositional phrase. _____

_____

_____

4. Begin with an infinitive verb. _____

_____

_____

5. Begin with a gerund verb. _____

_____

_____

6. Begin with an interjection. _____

_____

_____

Directions: Rewrite the sentence below, following the instruction provided. Use page 31 from the Writer's Notebook to help you.

The batter swung.

1. Begin with two adjectives. _____

_____

_____

2. Begin with a question. _____

_____

_____

3. Begin with a prepositional phrase. _____

_____

_____

4. Begin with an infinitive verb. _____

_____

_____

5. Begin with a gerund verb. _____

_____

_____

6. Begin with an interjection. _____

_____

_____

- ☐ Discuss the content of How to Construct a Paragraph in the Writer's Notebook (page 33). Explain to the students the importance of organization and clarity in getting across an idea. Words and sentences must be carefully chosen in order to express exactly what the writer desires.

- ☐ Collect paragraph examples from a variety of publications and bring them into the classroom. Share the writings with the students. Have them break down the components of the paragraphs. This can be a good small group activity.

- ☐ Recopy a student-written paragraph onto the board or overhead projector. (If possible, use a paragraph from a previous year's student or someone from another class; keep the paragraph anonymous.) As a class, proofread and edit the paragraph. Have each student or student group revise the proofread work. Compare the various results.

- ☐ Distribute Student Page 61. Instruct the students to write three supporting sentences between the first and last sentences (provided) of the paragraphs. Share and compare their results. (You might wish to provide an example before they work; however, this might also color their work, so it is not necessary.)

- ☐ Distribute Student Page 62 (six sheets). Each student will receive one sheet (or more if you choose). Instruct the students to write a paragraph from the provided topic, using the outline given on page 33 of the Writer's Notebook. Have the students take their paragraphs through the writing process. Share the finished products with the entire class or in small groups. If desired, have the class compare the paragraphs written on the same topic.

Additional Ideas/Notes

_____

_____

_____

_____

_____

_____

_____

_____

_____

Directions: Each pair of sentences is the first and last sentence of a paragraph. Write three supporting sentences in between each set of two to make two complete paragraphs.

1. First sentence: I have many reasons to feel proud of myself.

_____

_____

_____

_____

_____

_____

_____

_____

_____

Last sentence: Wouldn't you feel proud, too?

2. First sentence: A person can have a really good time at a baseball game.

_____

_____

_____

_____

_____

_____

_____

_____

_____

_____

_____

Last sentence: I wish we were at a game right now!

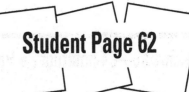

Directions: Using the guidelines for writing a paragraph (see the Writer's Notebook, page 33), write a five-sentence paragraph on the following topic. After writing a rough draft, get a response, edit, recopy, and proofread.

Topic: A New Pet

rough draft

_____

_____

_____

_____

_____

_____

_____

_____

final copy

_____

_____

_____

_____

_____

_____

_____

_____

Directions: Using the guidelines for writing a paragraph (see the Writer's Notebook, page 33), write a five-sentence paragraph on the following topic. After writing a rough draft, get a response, edit, recopy, and proofread.

Topic: Endangered Animals

rough draft

_____

_____

_____

_____

_____

_____

_____

final copy

_____

_____

_____

_____

_____

_____

_____

_____

_____

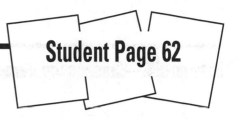

Directions: Using the guidelines for writing a paragraph (see the Writer's Notebook, page 33), write a five-sentence paragraph on the following topic. After writing a rough draft, get a response, edit, recopy, and proofread.

Topic: My Favorite Shoes

rough draft

_____

_____

_____

_____

_____

_____

_____

_____

final copy

_____

_____

_____

_____

_____

_____

_____

_____

Directions: Using the guidelines for writing a paragraph (see the Writer's Notebook, page 33), write a five-sentence paragraph on the following topic. After writing a rough draft, get a response, edit, recopy, and proofread.

Topic: Importance of Family

rough draft

_____

_____

_____

_____

_____

_____

_____

_____

final copy

_____

_____

_____

_____

_____

_____

_____

_____

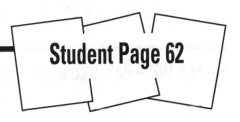

Directions: Using the guidelines for writing a paragraph (see the Writer's Notebook, page 33), write a five-sentence paragraph on the following topic. After writing a rough draft, get a response, edit, recopy, and proofread.

Topic: Beauty Is Only Skin Deep

rough draft

_____

_____

_____

_____

_____

_____

_____

final copy

_____

_____

_____

_____

_____

_____

_____

Directions: Using the guidelines for writing a paragraph (see the Writer's Notebook, page 33), write a five-sentence paragraph on the following topic. After writing a rough draft, get a response, edit, recopy, and proofread.

Topic: Computers Are Here to Stay

rough draft

_____

_____

_____

_____

_____

_____

_____

_____

final copy

_____

_____

_____

_____

_____

_____

_____

Lesson 20—Writing Quotations

- ☐ Discuss the importance of knowing the correct form for writing quotations.
- ☐ Present and discuss the pattern for writing quotations as described in the Writer's Notebook (page 34).
- ☐ Have the students listen to a recorded conversation, perhaps on video or one you make yourself. While listening, ask them to count the number of different quotations (each time a speaker takes a turn).
- ☐ Listen again, this time writing down what is said. The students will need to have it repeated several times to get it all. It will be a good idea to let them work in teams. Once it has been written, ask them to put in the appropriate quotation marks.
- ☐ Review synonyms for "said" in the Writer's Notebook (page 35).
- ☐ Employing duplicated pages from comic books and Sunday funnies, instruct the students to write the bubbled conversation in quotation marks, endeavoring, whenever possible, to use a substitute word for said.
- ☐ Distribute Student Page 63. Instruct the students to add quotation marks and other punctuation in the appropriate places. Here are the answers:

    1. "Clean your room immediately," ordered Bill's dad.
    2. "Stop wasting time," demanded the teacher.
    3. "I hate spinach," complained Tom.
    4. Jane asked, "May I please go to the movies?"
    5. The sign in the library said, "Quiet Please."
    6. Mary asked Jean, "May I borrow your green dress?"
    7. "Please answer the phone," requested Mom.
    8. "Where is your driver's license?" questioned the policeman.
    9. Mary said, "Did you read that book?"
    10. John suggested, "Let's have a party."

- ☐ Distribute Student Page 64 (two sheets). Instruct the students to write an original sentence quotation for each of the listed words (synonyms for said).
- ☐ Distribute Student Page 65 (two sheets). Instruct the students to write a discussion, using quotation marks. They should also incorporate (in quotes) the counter argument. See the directions on the page for further detail.
- ☐ Distribute Student Page 66. Instruct the students to write a dialogue, using quotes, for one of the listed pairs. If desired, have them take this dialogue through the writing process.
- ☐ Distribute Student Page 67. Instruct the students to choose one of the listed quotes to begin an original story. They should then complete the story, incorporating as many quotes as possible. For an extra challenge, have them determine how many of the listed quotes they can use in one story.

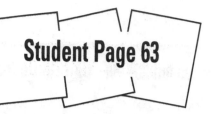

Directions: Read the sentences below. Show the exact words someone says by placing punctuation (period, comma, quotation marks) wherever necessary. Refer to page 34 in the Writer's Notebook for help.

1. Clean your room immediately ordered Bill's dad.

2. Stop wasting time demanded the teacher.

3. I hate spinach complained Tom.

4. Jane asked May I please go to the movies?

5. The sign in the library said Quiet Please.

6. Mary asked Jean May I borrow your green dress?

7. Please answer the phone requested Mom.

8. Where is your driver's license questioned the policeman.

9. Mary said Did you read that book?

10. John suggested Let's have a party.

Lesson 20B—Writing Quotations

Directions: Write a quotation for each of the following words, substitutes for the word "said."

Example: "May I go with you?" asked Mary.

1. admitted _____

2. agreed _____

3. announced _____

4. answered _____

5. argued _____

6. asked _____

7. bargained _____

8. boasted _____

9. complained _____

10. confided _____

11. cried _____

12. denied _____

13. exclaimed _____

14. explained _____

15. feared _____

16. giggled _____

17. laughed _____

18. lied _____

19. moaned _____

20. mumbled _____

21. nagged _____

22. objected _____

23. ordered _____

24. predicted _____

25. reassured _____

26. roared _____

27. scolded _____

28. screamed _____

29. shrieked _____

30. sobbed _____

31. stammered _____

32. threatened _____

33. vowed _____

34. wailed _____

35. warned _____

36. questioned _____

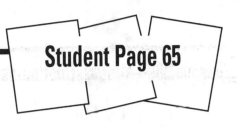

Lesson 20C—Discussion Quotations

Directions: Imagine you are trying to convince your parents to let you do one of the following things:

- Go to the mall
- Buy a new bike
- Swim in your neighbor's pool
- Go to the movies with a friend
- Learn to play an instrument
- Buy a dog
- Learn to drive a car

You are going to write a discussion on your chosen topic, using quotation marks. The discussion will take place between yourself and your mom and/or dad. Here are the steps to follow:

1. List your arguments for the topic (at least 3).

2. List possible arguments against the topic (at least 3).

3. Choose some of these synonyms for *said* to include in your discussion.

• added	• began	• objected
• answered	• claimed	• pleaded
• argued	• explained	• suggested
• asserted	• maintained	• pointed out
• responded	• stated	• proclaimed
• urged	• nagged	• reasoned
• asked	• noted	• replied

4. Use the information above and the outline on the next page to write an imaginary dialogue between you and your parent(s) on your chosen topic. Begin with, "Mom/Dad, may I please . . . ." After writing your rough draft, get a response and then revise, edit, recopy, and proofread your writing.

Pattern

Request and Argument for

"May I please . . .

Reply argument against

"

Argument for

"

Argument against

"

Argument for

"

Concluding statement

Lesson 20D—Writing a Conversation

Directions: Write a dialogue story between one of the following pairs. After writing your rough draft, get a response and then revise, edit, recopy, and proofread your writing.

- a star and the moon
- a bee and a rose
- a hand and a glove
- a cat and a mouse

- two peas in a pod
- an oak and an acorn
- the shore and the ocean
- a ball and a bat

_____

_____

_____

_____

_____

_____

_____

_____

_____

_____

_____

_____

_____

_____

_____

_____

Directions: Begin a story with one of the following quotations. As your story progresses, use other quotations. After writing your rough draft, get a response and then revise, edit, recopy, and proofread your writing.

Challenge: Incorporate as many of the following quotes as you can into your story.

"Fire! Fire!" screamed the frightened woman.

"Stop in the name of the law!" demanded the police officer.

"I can't breathe!" gasped the panic-stricken man.

"Three . . . two . . . one . . . Blast off!" announced the control tower.

"Land ho!" called the lookout boy atop the crow's nest of the clipper ship.

"Whooooo," was the mournful sound made by a lone owl in the dark forest.

"Sssssss," hissed the brightly colored snake hidden behind the rock.

"Bang!" echoed the sound of the gun as the race began.

_____

_____

_____

_____

_____

_____

_____

_____

_____

_____

_____

☐ Discuss the structure of a good story as outlined in the Writer's Notebook (page 36).

☐ Read a sample story or two to the class. It will be useful to read one humorous story and another suspenseful or dramatic one. Have the class discuss what you read, particularly the structure and components of the story. Ask them what makes the stories good or interesting.

☐ Follow these steps for writing a story:

1. Present students with a subject about which to write—for example, an adventure with friends. Instruct each to draw a picture about the subject. Afterwards, have them tell the class about their pictures and what is happening.

2. Using copies of pages 37–38 in the Writer's Notebook and the topic above, each student can write a preparatory description of the setting and characters in his story.

3. Employing copies of pages 39–42 in the Writer's Notebook and the work done on pages 37–38, each student can outline the events of his or her story.

4. Each student will draft his or her story. Encourage the use of the following:

descriptive words	sequential words
personification	similes
idioms	synonyms
alliteration	hyperboles
metaphors	transition words

   Stress the avoidance of the dead words listed in the Writer's Notebook (page 43).

5. Have the students share their work with a partner or small group, getting response from them. Use page 44 or 45 of the Writer's Notebook, if desired.

6. Instruct the students to revise and edit on the basis of the response and their own reviews.

7. Instruct the students to recopy their work carefully and to do a final proofreading.

8. Publish and/or share the stories.

☐ Duplicate Student Page 68 (four sheets) two times each. Cut out the separate boxes and place each group (people, places, ideas, and things) in different sacks or baskets. Have students draw one from each of the four bags. These can become their main character, setting, theme, and central object (around which the plot unfolds). Use corresponding forms from pages 36–45 of the Writer's Notebook to help. Publish and share when complete.

☐ Distribute Student Page 69 and one of the corresponding picture sheets to each student. Instruct them to follow the directions on page 69 in order to write a story.

People

Jim McConnell, farmer	Imogene Potts, artist	Buffy Alexander, teenager	Lily Okura, detective	Juan Martinez, lawyer	Cindy Smothers, 1st grader	Barnabus Eldridge, fisherman	Tyler Diamond, actor	Brenda Montoya, doctor
Andrea Taylor, teacher	Carl Saunders, carpenter	Kenny Walsh, baby	Sam Miller, quarterback	Gino Carelli, clown	Janet Weiss, dentist	Lola Phillips, rock star	Charlie Palmo, chef	K.C. Caruthers, magician

Places

park	seashore
desert island	forest
pond	Mars
mansion	abandoned shack
small farm	spaceship
ocean liner	circus
secret room	school
hospital	office building
theater	stadium

Themes

Home is where the heart is.	Never judge a book by its cover.
Beauty is only skin deep.	Birds of a feather flock together.
Look before you leap.	Beauty is in the eye of the beholder.
Don't cry over spilt milk.	The pen is mightier than the sword.
You can't teach an old dog new tricks.	A watched pot never boils.
All that glitters is not gold.	People in glass houses should not throw stones.
Too many cooks spoil the broth.	A rolling stone gathers no moss.
He who laughs last, laughs best.	Nothing ventured, nothing gained.
A stitch in time saves nine.	A bird in the hand is worth two in the bush.

Objects

toothbrush	diamond ring
magic wand	storybook
treasure map	pencil
hamburger	bottle of root beer
magnifying glass	guitar
telephone	radio headset
painting	pine tree
fishing pole	basketball
teddy bear	bucket

Directions: Study pages 36 and 39–42 of the Writer's Notebook. Then study the picture on the following page.* Think about a story the picture tells, as well as the characters and setting. Write some of your rough ideas on the lines below. Use copies of the pages in the Writer's Notebook (pages 37-38) to help you.

To write your story, do the following:

1. From information above and in the Writer's Notebook, write a rough draft. Try to avoid dead words (page 43).

2. Get a response from a classmate.

3. Revise and edit.

4. Recopy for a final draft.

5. Proofread for errors.

*Note to the teacher: Provide one picture per student.

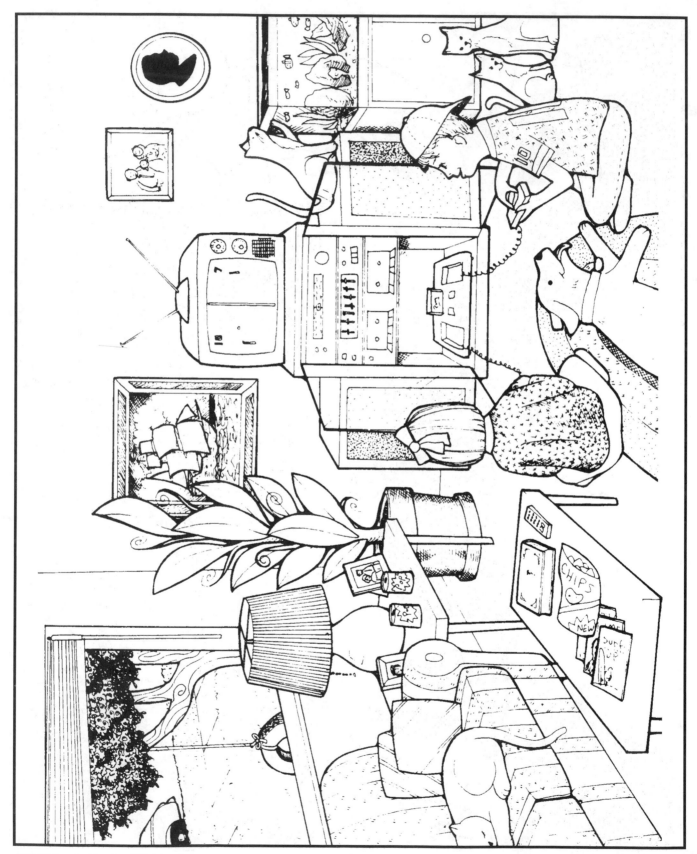

- ☐ Discuss the correct letter and envelop formats for a friendly letter, located in the Writer's Notebook (pages 46 and 47).
- ☐ Discuss different types of friendly letters (Student Pages 70, 71, 72, 73, 74, and 75).
- ☐ Discuss the value of including something like one of the following with a friendly letter:
    - comic clipping
    - picture of oneself or a pet
    - homemade puzzle or tic-tac-toe board
    - sample of perfume on a cottonball
    - unusual leaf
    - joke
    - drawing or piece of art
- ☐ Let the students tell you when and if each of these items—and others—might be appropriate to include.
- ☐ As a class, brainstorm for and discuss the types of writing and expression one might include in a friendly letter.
- ☐ Distribute each of Student Pages 70 through 75, one at a time. Each one outlines a different type of friendly letter. Have the students write each type according to the directions on the pages.

Additional Ideas/Notes

_____

_____

_____

_____

_____

_____

_____

_____

_____

Directions: Write a thank you letter to someone who has given you something. Take the letter through the writing process. (The space below can be used for your first draft.) Be sure to add something personal to your thanks, such as how you use the gift. Address an envelope, as well. Use the letter and envelope forms in the Writer's Notebook (pages 46 and 47) to help you.

Date _____

Dear _____,

Paragraph 1: Mention what was received, how it will be used, and/or its benefit. Also tell of your appreciation.

Paragraph 2: Tell some family news.

Paragraph 3: Thank the giver again for her kindness and express your hope to see her soon.

Love,

_____

Signature

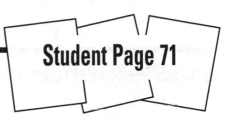

Directions: Write a letter to your parents about what is happening at school. Take the letter through the writing process. (The space below can be used for your first draft.) Address an envelope, as well. Use the letter and envelope forms in the Writer's Notebook (pages 46 and 47) to help you.

Date _____

Dear _____,

Paragraph 1+: Mention new or exciting happenings in two or more areas of school such as reading, writing, math, science, social studies, and physical education. Tell about trips, guests, assemblies, and other interesting and novel happenings.

Last Paragraph: Invite your parents to visit your class.

Love,

_____

Signature

Directions: Write a letter to a new pen pal. Take the letter through the writing process. (The space below can be used for your first draft.) Address an envelope, as well. Use the letter and envelope forms in the Writer's Notebook (pages 46 and 47) to help you.

Date _____

Dear _____,

Paragraph 1: Introduce yourself, telling your age, grade, home, family life, and where you grew up.

Paragraph 2: Tell about some of your favorite activities and interests.

Paragraph 3: Tell about your friends and/or people you admire.

Paragraph 4: Ask for a reply in which your pen pal will tell something about himself.

Your new friend,

_____

Signature

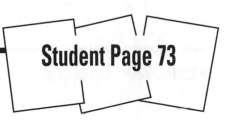
Directions: Write a letter to your teacher or principal stating good things that have happened or are happening in the classroom and/or school. Take the letter through the writing process. (The space below can be used for your first draft.) Address an envelope, as well. Use the letter and envelope forms in the Writer's Notebook (pages 46 and 47) to help you.

Date _____

Dear _____,

Paragraph 1: State good things that have happened and their benefits.

Paragraph 2: State how life at school has improved.

Paragraph 3: State your hopes for the future as related to the good happenings.

Sincerely,

_____

Signature

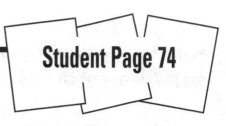

Lesson 22E—"Teacher Reacher" Complaint Letter

Directions: Write a letter to your teacher or principal about something to improve in the classroom or school. Take the letter through the writing process. (The space below can be used for your first draft.) Address an envelope, as well. Use the letter and envelope forms in the Writer's Notebook (pages 46 and 47) to help you.

Date _____

Dear _____,

Paragraph 1: State your concern and any negative effect.

Paragraph 2: Suggest changes, in detail.

Paragraph 3: Discuss benefits of your suggestions.

Thank you for your attention.

Sincerely,

_____

Signature

Directions: Pretend you are giving a party. Fill in the important information on the worksheet below. Next, fold a standard-size paper in half and center the information on the inside right-hand side. Now, decorate the front fold of the invitation and, if desired, also decorate the page where the invitation is written. Properly address an envelope, using the envelope form in the Writer's Notebook (page 47) to help you.

Date: _____

Place: _____

Time: _____

Details *(type of party, dress, etc.):*

_____

_____

_____

_____

_____

_____

_____

_____

_____

_____

_____

R.S.V.P. *(telephone number):*_____

Mention your hope that the person will come.

❑ Discuss the proper form for writing a business letter and review it in the Writer's Notebook (page 48).

❑ Discuss the different types of business letters. Three types are provided on Student Pages 76, 77, and 78.

❑ Present Student Page 76 and review the guidelines for ordering merchandise in a business letter. Instruct the students to write a business letter order, using Writer's Notebook page 48 and Student Page 76. Have the students address an envelope for their letters according to the form on page 47 in the Writer's Notebook.

❑ Present Student Page 77 and review the guidelines for filing a complaint in a business letter. Instruct the students to write a business letter complaint, using Writer's Notebook page 48 and Student Page 77. Have the students address an envelope for their letters according to the form on page 47 in the Writer's Notebook.

❑ Present Student Page 78 and review the guidelines for writing a letter of praise in a business letter format. Instruct the students to write a business letter of praise, using Writer's Notebook page 48 and Student Page 78. Have the students address an envelope for their letters according to the form on page 47 in the Writer's Notebook.

❑ As responses are sent in reply to the students' business letters, have them share the letters in class. Collect copies of the originals with their responses in a class book.

Additional Ideas/Notes

_____

_____

_____

_____

_____

_____

_____

_____

Lesson 23A—Writing Business Letters (Ordering Merchandise)

Directions: Use the information below and the outline on the following page to write a business letter ordering a T-shirt. (The T-shirt and company are fictional.) Take your letter through the writing process. Address an envelope. (Use pages 47 and 48 in the Writer's Notebook to help you.)

Bright Color T-shirts

colors: red, yellow, blue, green, or pink
sizes: small, medium, or large
cost: $5.95 each

Send check or money order to:
Fabulous Fashions
629 West Elm St.
City, State 97250
Allow 4 weeks for delivery.

Lesson 23A—Writing Business Letters (Ordering Merchandise) (*cont.*)

Your Name   _____

Your Address   _____

Your City, State and Zip   _____

Date   _____

_____   Name of Star/Company

_____   Address of Star/Company

_____   Star/Company City, State and Zip

Dear Sir or Madam:

Paragraph 1: State what you are ordering and all pertinent details such as color, size, and method of payment.

Paragraph 2: State your full address.

Sincerely,

_____

Signature

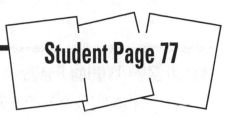

Lesson 23B—Writing Business Letters (Complaints)

Directions: Use the outline below to write a business letter complaining about something. (For example, imagine a cereal box was missing its free prize. What might you complain about?) Take your letter through the writing process. Address an envelope. (Use pages 47 and 48 in the Writer's Notebook to help you.)

Your Name _____

Your Address _____

Your City, State and Zip _____

Date _____

_____ *Name of Star/Company*

_____ *Address of Star/Company*

_____ *Star/Company City, State and Zip*

Dear Sir or Madam:

Paragraph 1: Explain your complaint.

Paragraph 2: Explain what you would like to have done to rectify the situation.

Thank you for your attention to this matter.

Sincerely,

_____

Signature

Lesson 23C—Writing Business Letters (Praise)

Directions: Choose a favorite music star or movie and write a fan letter. Use the addresses below and the outline on the following page. Take your letter through the writing process. Address an envelope. (Use pages 47 and 48 in the Writer's Notebook to help you.)

Addresses for Fan Letters:

Television

NBC TV 30 Rockefeller Plaza, New York, NY 10020

ABC TV 1330 Avenue of Americas, New York, NY 10019

CBS TV 51 West 52nd Street, New York, NY 10009

PBS 425 L'Enfant Plaza Southwest, Washington, DC 20024

Music

A&M Records, Inc. 1416 La Brea Avenue, Hollywood, CA 90028

RCA Records 30 Music Square West, Nashville, TN 37203

CBS (Columbia) Records, Inc. 51 West 52nd Street, New York, NY 10009

Warner Bros. Records, Inc. 4000 Warner Blvd., Burbank, CA

Movies

Columbia Pictures Columbia Plaza, Burbank, CA 91505

Disney Productions 500 South Buena Vista St., Burbank, CA 91521

Allied Artists 9200 Sunset Blvd., Los Angeles, CA 90069

20th Century Fox 10201 West Pico Blvd., Los Angeles, CA 90064

Lucas Film 3855 Lankersheim Blvd., Hollywood, CA 91604

Paramount Pictures 5451 Melrose St., Los Angeles, CA 90038

Lesson 23C—Writing Business Letters (Praise) (*cont.*)

Your Name   _____

Your Address   _____

Your City, State and Zip   _____

Date   _____

_____ Name of Star/Company

_____ Address of Star/Company

_____ Star/Company City, State and Zip

Dear _____:

Paragraphs 1 and 2: Tell what you like about the person/company.

Paragraph 3: Tell how the person/company has affected your life.

Paragraph 4: Ask for an autograph (if a person).

                                          Sincerely,

                                          _____

                                          Signature

❑ Define *contrast* and *comparison* for the class or have them look up the words in their dictionaries.

❑ Discuss the need to write contrast and comparison papers to come to logical solutions to problems or issues.

❑ As a class, orally contrast and compare two things in the classroom or two sides of one thing. Encourage the students to describe what the process of contrasting and comparing entails.

❑ With students, work through Student Page 79 (two sheets). First, brainstorm for the good and the bad points of television. Then write paragraphs as outlined on the second sheet. This will be the comparison and contrast paper.

❑ Using Student Page 80 (three sheets), have the students repeat the procedure as above but this time independently with a topic of their choice. A list of topics to choose from is provided for those who would like some ideas. The class as a whole can brainstorm for other topics to add to the list.

❑ Refer to appropriate transition words (page 15, Writer's Notebook) and the outline and pattern for contrast and comparison writing in the Writer's Notebook (pages 49 and 50).

Additional Ideas/Notes

_____

_____

_____

_____

_____

_____

_____

_____

_____

_____

Directions: Complete the chart below on the topic of television. One the left side, write the good points of television, in your opinion. On the right side, write the bad points. Then, take your ideas and incorporate them into paragraphs, using the form on the next page. Take your work through the writing process.

Topic: Television: Good or Bad?

Good Points (and examples)	Bad Points (and examples)

Lesson 24A—Contrast and Comparison Writing (*cont.*)

Paragraph 1: Tell the good points about television and give examples.

Paragraph 2: Tell the bad points about television and give examples.

Paragraph 3: Briefly summarize Paragraphs 1 and 2.

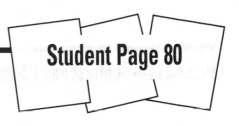

Lesson 24B—Contrast and Compare

Directions: From the list below, choose an issue to compare and contrast. Complete the chart on the next page. Use the information for writing a comparison and contrast paper (third sheet). Take your work through the writing process.

Single subjects:

- school
- brothers and sisters
- sports
- movies
- computers
- growing up
- being your age

Double subjects:

- hamburgers vs. hot dogs
- baseball vs. football
- school vs. vacation
- cars vs. buses
- math vs. science
- Halloween vs. Christmas
- summer vs. winter

Add other topics for comparison.

_____   _____

_____   _____

_____   _____

_____   _____

_____   _____

_____   _____

_____   _____

_____   _____

_____   _____

_____   _____

Topic: _____

Good Points or Likenesses
(and examples)

Bad Points or Differences
(and examples)

_____   _____

_____   _____

_____   _____

_____   _____

_____   _____

_____   _____

_____   _____

_____   _____

_____   _____

_____   _____

_____   _____

_____   _____

_____   _____

_____   _____

_____   _____

_____   _____

_____   _____

_____   _____

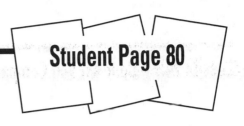

Lesson 24B—Contrast and Compare (*cont.*)

Topic:

Paragraph 1: Tell the good points or likenessess and give examples.

_____

_____

_____

_____

_____

_____

Paragraph 2: Tell the bad points or differences and give examples.

_____

_____

_____

_____

_____

Paragraph 3: Briefly summarize Paragraphs 1 and 2.

_____

_____

_____

_____

_____

☐ Discuss the importance of cause and effect writing in order for one to analyze situations and possibly to come up with solutions.

☐ Discuss the pattern for cause and effect writing in the Writer's Notebook (page 51). Distribute page 51 to the students.

☐ Read the following paragraph to the class:

The cost of attending college is very high and growing higher; therefore, fewer students are going to college than in the past. These students are not receiving the benefits of higher education. The result is that fewer people are available to enter highly skilled professions, and fewer people will be able to command high salaries and to enjoy a better standard of living.

Using the above paragraph, ask students to respond to the following:

- What is the cause?

- What transition word is used to go from cause to effect?

- What are the effects?

☐ Ask students to write their own cause and effect paragraph, using Student Page 81. Cause and effect ideas include the following:

• preparing for a test	• a lion's escape
• a terrible storm	• an earthquake
• driving without seat belts	• not doing homework
• not brushing teeth	• no exercise

Have the students brainstorm for other topics before they begin.

Additional Ideas/Notes

_____

_____

_____

_____

_____

_____

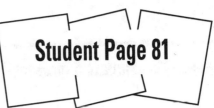

Lesson 25—Cause and Effect Writing

Directions: The following outline can be used to write a cause and effect paper. This type of writing tells what happens and gives its natural consequences or results. Sometimes, solutions to a resulting problem are also provided.

Write your rough draft below. Then, take your work through the writing process.

Title: _____

Paragraph 1: Describe the incident (the cause). Be sure to state specifically what happens.

_____

_____

_____

_____

Paragraph 2: Describe the result or results of the cause, clearly stating each one. If the results are very different, you may need more than one paragraph to do this.

_____

_____

_____

_____

_____

Paragraph 3: Suggest a remedy to the effects if they are negative.

_____

_____

_____

_____

❑ Discuss the importance of recognizing and writing about a subject from different points of view.

❑ For example, each of the following sentences expresses a different point of view about watching television.

- Teacher's point of view: Students watch television instead of doing schoolwork.

- Student's point of view: Television is relaxing.

- Parent's point of view: My son/daughter neglects being helpful when watching television.

❑ Discuss the outline for writing a point of view paper. It can be found on page 52 of the Writer's Notebook. Distribute it to the class.

❑ As a class, discuss various points of view for the following situation. A soccer game is being played between a group of girls and a group of boys. Discuss possible viewpoints, including a boy, a girl, an adult watching the game, and a teacher. You may consider different or other viewpoints, as well.

❑ Distribute Student Page 82 to guide students in writing a point of view paper about one of the following from at least two points of view:

1. dog chases a boy on a bike
    a. dog's point of view
    b. cat's point of view
    c. point of view of a balloon caught in a tree
    d. boy's point of view
    e. mother's point of view
    f. rescuer's point of view

2. use of calculators in math class
    a. teacher's point of view
    b. student's point of view
    c. school district point of view
    d. principal's point of view
    e. parent's point of view
    f. calculator manufacturer's point of view

3. Use of animals in medical experimentation
    a. scientist's point of view
    b. humanistic point of view
    c. monkey's point of view

❑ As an extension, turn different points of view on the same topic into a mini-play, with each person or group espousing his own point of view.

Lesson 26—How to Express a Point of View

Directions: Use this worksheet to express different points of view. Choose your topic and then write about it from at least two different points of view. Take your work through the writing process.

Topic: _____

Viewpoint 1

_____

_____

_____

_____

_____

_____

_____

_____

Viewpoint 2

_____

_____

_____

_____

_____

_____

_____

_____

Use additional paper for more points of view.

☐ Define *opinion* and *editorial* for the class. An opinion is a conclusion, view, or judgment held by one or more individuals. An editorial is a piece of writing that expresses and supports an opinion.

☐ Discuss the value of being able to express one's ideas about problems and issues. Tell the students that the most important thing when expressing an opinion is clarity.

☐ Distribute page 53 from the Writer's Notebook. Discuss.

☐ Discuss possible subjects on which to write an opinion:

- Should calculators be used in classrooms?
- Should teenagers have a curfew time on Saturday night?
- Should a person experiment with drugs?
- Should animals be used for scientific experimentation?
- Should television programs be rated?

☐ Allow the students to brainstorm for other topics.

☐ Choose one topic and have the students share as many opinions about it as they can (not necessarily their own). Point out how there are as many opinions as there are people in the world.

☐ Distribute Student Page 83. Ask each student, pair, or student group to list all the opinions they can think of concerning the given topic. Afterwards, share as a class.

☐ Discuss paragraph development for writing opinions as presented in the Writer's Notebook (page 53).

☐ Assign students to write a paper expressing a strong opinion they hold, using Student Page 84.

☐ Share some editorials from your local newspaper. Distribute Student Page 85. Instruct the students to write their own editorials, using the outline on the page. They can then mail their editorials to the newspaper. Watch the paper for possible printings of their work.

Additional Ideas/Notes

_____

_____

_____

_____

_____

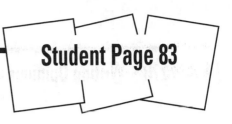

Lesson 27A—Opinions

Directions: On the page below, write as many opinions about the given topic as you can. The opinions you write do not have to be your own.

Topic: modern music

Opinions:

Directions: Choose an idea or problem about which you have a very strong opinion. Write your ideas on the page below. Take your work through the writing process.

Topic: _____

Paragraph 1: Give a detailed description of the issue or problem.

Paragraph 2: State why this issue or problem is important to consider.

Paragraph 3: Present the best solution, in your opinion.

Paragraph 4: Write the benefits of the change that will be brought about by your solution.

Directions: Write an editorial to your local newspaper. To do so, follow these steps:

1. Choose a social or political issue about which you have strong feelings and a clear opinion.

2. Brainstorm your ideas about the topic and your opinion.

3. Organize your ideas in an outline.

4. Write your ideas in a letter to the editor.

5. Follow the writing process to complete your letter.

6. Mail your letter to the local paper.

Use the space below to write and organize your ideas.

_____

_____

_____

_____

_____

_____

_____

_____

_____

_____

_____

_____

_____

_____

_____

_____

☐ Discuss what a *summary* is, a brief statement of important points of a piece of writing.

☐ Distribute copies of a current newspaper article or current event and discuss how to summarize it. Summarize it as a class. Tell the students to consider the following:

- List the important ideas in one's own words.

- Combine ideas wherever possible.

- Keep it brief.

☐ Instruct the students to bring in newspaper articles. (Bring in several yourself for those who do not.) Distribute Student Page 86 and have the students complete it as outlined.

☐ Distribute page 54 in the Writer's Notebook. Have the students keep it with their other Writer's Notebook pages as a reminder of how to write a summary.

☐ Discuss the value of summarizing when researching for a report.

☐ Distribute Student Page 87. Instruct the students to write a detailed paragraph from one of the provided summary statements.

☐ Distribute Student Page 88. Instruct the students to write a summary of one of the listed fairy tales. Afterwards, compare the summaries to determine how alike they are. As a class, review the value of the items included in the summaries.

☐ As an alternative to the above, have each student secretly choose a fairy tale or other story with which the class is probably familiar. Have them summarize it without naming names. Share the summaries with the class to see if the story title can be determined. A good summary will allow this.

Additional Ideas/Notes

_____

_____

_____

_____

_____

_____

Lesson 28A—Writing a Summary

Directions: Choose a newspaper article and use the following worksheet to write a summary of that article. Staple the article to your summary.

List the important facts in your own words.

_____

_____

_____

_____

_____

_____

Combine the above facts wherever possible.

_____

_____

_____

_____

_____

_____

Rewrite the above ideas in a brief, clear way.

Directions: Read each of the summaries below. Expand one of them into a more detailed paragraph from which the summary might have come. Be sure that the summary tells the most important thing about your new paragraph.

Summaries:

1. We must keep our national parks clean for future generations.
2. Parenting is strenuous but rewarding work.
3. School is difficult but worth the effort.
4. It is best to have a career that one enjoys.
5. Pets take a lot of time and care.

My choice: _____

Paragraph:

_____

_____

_____

_____

_____

_____

_____

_____

_____

_____

_____

_____

_____

_____

_____

_____

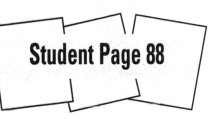
Directions: Choose one of the fairy tales listed below. Write a summary of its important events. Include everything that is necessary to tell the main points of the story. Delete all unnecessary details.

Fairy Tales:

- *Little Red Riding Hood*
- *Goldilocks and the Three Bears*
- *The Princess and the Pea*
- *Jack and the Beanstalk*
- *Beauty and the Beast*
- *Cinderella*
- *Thumbelina*
- *Pinocchio*

_____

_____

_____

_____

_____

_____

_____

_____

_____

_____

_____

_____

_____

_____

Lesson 29—Conducting and Writing Interviews

Teacher's Guide

❑ Videotape some televised interviews and show them to the class. Ask the students to describe the interviewing techniques they see. Have them consider and discuss what makes a good interviewer.

❑ Discuss prerequisites to conducting an interview:

- Make an advanced appointment.
- Be well prepared in advance with specific questions to be asked.
- Ask who, what, where, when, why, and how.
- Group together questions that deal with the same topic.
- When an individual says something interesting or that requires more detail, ask follow-up questions.
- When preparing questions, leave spaces to write the person's response.
- Thank the person for the interview.

❑ A number of interview question topics have been provided on page 57 of the Writer's Notebook. Allow students to add others on a continuing basis.

❑ Allow students to interview a classmate, using Student Page 89 (two sheets).

❑ Assign students to interview an adult they know, following patterns for conducting and writing an interview in the Writer's Notebook (pages 55 and 56).

❑ Invite a guest into the classroom for the whole class to interview. Prepare ahead of time. Have each student write about the interview, retelling what was said. (This can also be used as a quotation mark or summarizing activity.) Send a class thank you letter to the guest.

Additional Ideas/Notes

_____

_____

_____

_____

_____

_____

_____

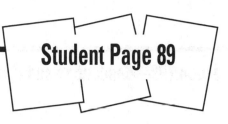

Lesson 29—Conducting and Writing Interviews

Directions: Choose a classmate to interview. Remember to make an advance appointment for the interview. (Your teacher may arrange this time.) Bring this worksheet, a pencil, and something on which to write. Be polite and thank your classmate for the interview.

Personal Information

- What is your name and age?
- Where were you born?

Family and Friends

- How many people are in your family?
- What is something you really like about your family?
- Who are your favorite friends?
- Why do you like them?

School

- What are your favorite school subjects? Why?
- Which subjects do you dislike? Why?

Interests

- What are your hobbies? Why did you choose them?

Future Plans

- What are your plans for the future?

Directions: Using the information on the previous page, write the results of your interview. Take your work through the writing process.

Paragraph 1: Include personal information.

Paragraph 2: Discuss family and friends.

Paragraph 3: Discuss school.

Paragraph 4: Discuss interests.

Paragraph 5: Discuss future plans.

Teacher's Guide

☐ Distribute to each student a duplicated, current news article from the daily paper. Read it together.

☐ Discuss the characteristics of a newspaper article:

- Headline, byline, and dateline

 headline is brief but dramatic/eye-catching

 byline tells name of writer

 dateline tells when action took place

- First part of the article tells who, what, and where the action took place.

- Subsequent sentences of paragraphs give details and tell the how and why.

☐ Distribute pages 58 and 59 in the Writer's Notebook. They provide students with guidelines for writing news articles. On a continuing basis, have the students add headlines to page 58 which they find to be particularly good.

☐ Use page 58 of the Writer's Notebook to help track information in a published news article. Can the students find all the components? Have them discuss the value of the article and how it might be improved, if possible.

☐ Present students with Student Page 90 (two sheets), which gives them facts about a new "Classics" program initiated at Stewart Elementary School. Assist students to write a news article about this event, using the second sheet of Student Page 90.

☐ Other possible topics for writing newspaper articles (Student Page 90, sheet two) include the following:

- school show or event
- school trip
- sports event
- party or social gathering

☐ Discuss headlines with the students and brainstorm for some interesting ones. Imaginary headlines might include the following:

- Worldwide Peace Treaty Signed
- U.F.O. Lands in Nebraska
- Cure Found for Deadly Disease
- New Invention Changes Modern Life

☐ Distribute Student Page 91. On it, students can experiment with illustrations that correspond to a news article.

Directions: Read the following facts. Then use these facts to write a news article on the next sheet. Pages 58 and 59 in the Writer's Notebook can help you.

- Principal Rose West announced today that Stewart School is now experimenting with a new Classical Studies Program.

- Three seminar teachers have been hired for this program.

- Seminar teachers take students in small groups to discuss in-depth areas of the curriculum.

- Students must leave the classroom for the seminar.

- Classroom teachers and seminar teachers work together in developing the subject matter.

- Teacher aides have been hired to assist students in the classroom.

- Basics are still most important in the curriculum.

- Homework is required.

- Program will be evaluated after three years.

_____

_____

_____

_____

_____

_____

_____

_____

_____

_____

_____

_____

Lesson 30A—Writing a Newspaper Article (*cont.*)

Directions: On the basis of the facts presented on the previous page, use the following outline to write a news article. Take your article through the writing process.

Headline _____

Byline_____

Dateline_____

Paragraph 1: who, what, and where

Paragraph 2+: how and why, organized logically

Final Paragraph: conclusion (summary, future plans, or other)

Lesson 30B—Illustrating a News Article

Directions: Draw a picture of one of the dramatic events listed below or choose an event from your own imagination. Write a newspaper article about the event, using the form outlined below.

- fire
- volcanic eruption
- invasion by aliens
- baseball game
- plane crash

Picture

Headline _____

Byline _____

Dateline _____

Paragraph 1: who, what, and where

Paragraph 2+: how and why, organized logically

Last Paragraph: conclusion

☐ Discuss the outline for writing a book report provided in the Writer's Notebook, page 60. Have the students add ideas to the sheet on a continuing basis.

☐ Using Student Page 92 (two sheets), instruct the students to write a book report on a book recently read. This is a standard form for a book report and includes all the primary information as well as the student's opinion.

☐ There are many other ways to do a book report. Ideas include the following:

- writing book jacket copy
- writing book advertisements
- writing news articles about the life and/or experiences of the main character
- making a poster collage about the main character or events
- writing/drawing a story map
- writing an "interview" of the main character
- rewriting the ending

☐ Include these ideas on page 60 of the Writer's Notebook.

☐ Ask the class to brainstorm for other interesting ways to write a book report. Assign some of their ideas.

Additional Ideas/Notes

_____

_____

_____

_____

_____

_____

_____

_____

_____

_____

Directions: Use the following form to write a book report on a recently read book. Write your rough draft on these pages and then take your work through the writing process.

Title: _____

Paragraph 1: title, author, illustrator, copyright, and genre (fiction, nonfiction, mystery, biography, etc.)

Paragraph 2: main characters, names, appearances, and how they act

Paragraph 3: time period and setting

Paragraph 4: brief discussion of plot and theme or main idea

Paragraph 5: personal opinion and recommendation

☐ Discuss the form for making an outline provided in the Writer's Notebook, pages 61 and 62.

☐ You might wish to review summaries before beginning outlines.

☐ Distribute the short account about the violin on Student Page 93 (two sheets). As a class, make an outline of the article, using the guidelines on the second sheet.

☐ Distribute page 63 from the Writer's Notebook. Let students know that a story web is a kind of outline. It can be used for gathering and collating ideas. Share with the students this sample web.

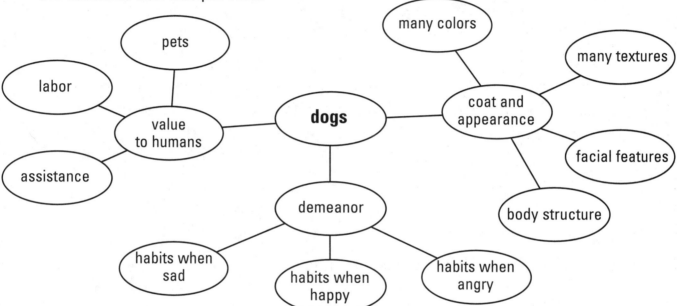

☐ Have student teams write outlines from other written material. They can exchange their outlines among the groups and then write articles based on the outlines given. The writers can then compare their versions with the originals.

☐ Practice making outlines on any given topics. Use the outline form provided on pages 61 and 62 of the Writer's Notebook.

Additional Ideas/Notes

_____

_____

_____

_____

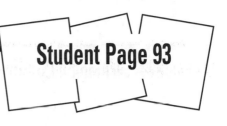
Directions: Read the article below. Then outline the article on the next page.

The Violin

The violin belongs to the violin family which includes the viola, cello, and string bass. The violin is the smallest but most popular instrument of the family. The violin family belongs to a large group of instruments called stringed instruments. The violin was brought into the orchestra about 1600. However, the origin of the violin was the rebec, an instrument of India.

The violin is made of fine wood and possesses four strings. It is held under the chin and rests on the left shoulder. It is played by drawing a fine horsehair bo across the strings. Different tones are made as the fingers of the left hand press at various places on the finger band.

The finest violin is the Stradivarius made by Antonio Stradivari. Several hundred of his violins made in the early 1700s are still used today and treasured by their owners.

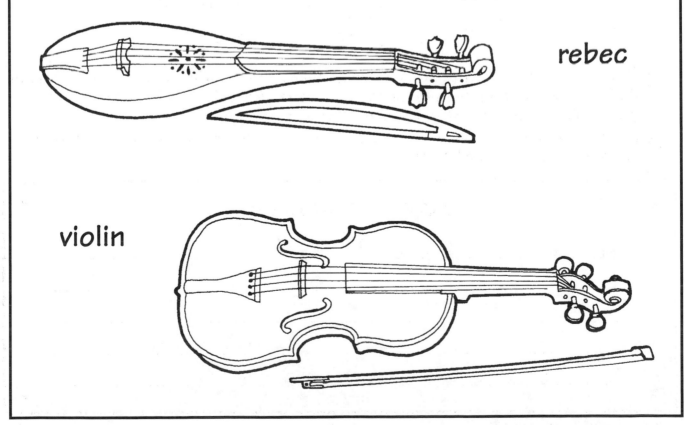

rebec

violin

Title: _____

I. Violin Family and Origin

    A. _____

        1. _____

        2. _____

    B. _____

        1. _____

        2. _____

II. Construction of Violin and How It Is Played

    A. _____

    B. _____

        1. _____

        2. _____

        3. _____

III. The Stradivarius

    A. _____

    B. _____

Lesson 33—Completing an Application

☐ Discuss the importance of filling out an application completely and accurately. Consider what might happen if one does not, as well as the benefits of doing it right. Let the students know that all of the following matter on an application:

- neatness and legibility
- spelling
- accuracy and honesty
- completeness
- information included

☐ Review the rules for filling out an application found in the Writer's Notebook, page 64.

☐ On the basis of the rules outlined in the Writer's Notebook (page 64), assign Student Page 94. Afterwards, share and discuss.

☐ Using Student Page 95, have each student fill in an imaginary application for employment.

☐ For fun, have the students write applications of their own.

☐ If possible, collect some job applications from local businesses. Duplicate them for the students to fill in for experience's sake.

Additional Ideas/Notes

_____

_____

_____

_____

_____

_____

_____

_____

_____

_____

Directions: Fill out the following application. Be sure to print and to fill in each space.

School File Information

_____ _____
Last Name   First   Middle   Grade

Name of Parent _____ _____
                                           Birthdate

Address _____
                                          Sex

Phone _____
                                        Race

Emergency Phone _____

Parent Occupation _____

Family Doctor _____

Phone _____

Daily Schedule

Period
Subject
Teacher
Room

Burger Palace Job Application

Name: _____

Address: _____

Phone Number: _____

> **Education:** _____
>
> _____
>
> _____
>
> _____

> **Work experience:** _____
>
> _____
>
> _____
>
> _____

Available hours to work: _____

> **Why you want this job:** _____
>
> _____
>
> _____
>
> _____

> **Future job plans:** _____
>
> _____
>
> _____
>
> _____

Lesson 34—Writing a Resumé

❑ Define resumé for the students and explain its purpose.

❑ Discuss the importance of being able to write a good resumé in order to obtain a worthwhile job.

❑ Review the outline for writing a resumé, found in the Writer's Notebook (page 65).

❑ Assign students to select a job for which they would like to apply and then to write a corresponding resumé, following the guidelines presented on Student Page 96. If desired, have small groups or the whole class review the resumés and their likelihood to earn the job. (Let the students know that the information on this activity should be imaginary. They are very unlikely to have current education and experience for their imagined careers!)

❑ If you are comfortable doing so, share your resumé with your students. Ask parents to do the same.

❑ Have the students write an accurate resumé of their true experience.

Additional Ideas/Notes

_____

_____

_____

_____

_____

_____

_____

_____

_____

_____

_____

Directions: Fill in appropriate information on the page below and the next. Then follow the writing process to rewrite the information into a good, job-getting resumé. Use Writer's Notebook page 65 as a reference.

_____

Name

_____

Street Number and Name

_____

City

_____

State and Zip

_____

Telephone Number

Paragraph 1: Job Objectives

Paragraph 2: Personal Information

Paragraph 3: Educational Background

Paragraph 4: Work Experience

Paragraph 5: References

Lesson 35—Guides to Editing and Proofreading

☐ Introduce the editing checklist and correcting symbols from the Writer's Notebook, pages 66 and 67. Review each of the items on the list so that the students are sure what they mean.

☐ Present Student Page 97 for the students to edit and proofread, using pages 66 and 67 from the Writer's Notebook.

☐ Distribute other student and published writing for editing and proofreading practice. Have the students compare their findings.

☐ Have the students compare revisions they make from the same edited copy. For example, edit a paragraph as a class and then instruct each student to revise it on his or her own. Share and compare the revisions to see the many ways in which a piece of writing can be edited. Stress, however, that the rules of spelling and grammar always apply.

☐ Be sure to include editing and proofreading as a part of most writing assignments, except for those that are intended to be merely brainstorms and drafts.

Additional Ideas/Notes

_____

_____

_____

_____

_____

_____

_____

_____

_____

_____

_____

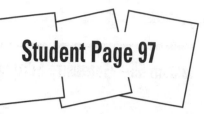

Directions: Mark errors in the story below, using the proofreading symbols provided on page 66 of your Writer's Notebook.

The Fire Dragon

Once upon a time there was an Island called Ishmar was prosperous and peaceful but one day an evil wizard came down and awoke up the Ancient Fire Dragon. With the dragon he runed haveck on Ishmar, he burned the town destroyed their fleat and wrecked the crops. Then the Partha, an Ancient water dragon, scooped up water as much water as it could and put out the First Dragon fires, but it couldn't destroy the Fire Dragon. That was when the six wizards of Ishmar their powers joined, killed the wizard and sealed the Fire Dragon in a ruby. Then life slowly is Ishmar returned normal to, but they never forgot the wizards or the pastha.

Lesson 36—Writing Poetry

☐ Read several examples of poetry to the students, including some they might not usually think of as poetry, such as Dr. Seuss books and music lyrics.

☐ Display many different types of poems around the classroom. Include both published and student-written examples, as well as some of your own. Add interesting colors and displays around the poetry to draw attention to it. You might wish to collect poetry around a theme and to display it with some thematic objects.

☐ Discuss two general categories of poetry, rhyming and non-rhyming. Share examples of both. A good source of poetry for students is *The Random House Book of Poetry for Children,* edited by Jack Prelutsky (Random House, 1983).

☐ Refer to and briefly discuss patterns for writing these popular types of poetry:

- cinquain
- haiku
- tanka
- couplet
- ode
- limerick

These are presented in the Writer's Notebook, pages 68–73.

☐ Distribute each of Student Pages 98, 99, 100, 101, 102, and 103, one at a time. Each one presents a type of poetry and provides a writing assignment. Allow the students plenty of time to create their verses. Also encourage the sharing of their poetry.

☐ Collect the samples of student poetry and put them into student or class poetry books.

☐ Allow students many opportunities for writing poems in the place of more traditional writing assignments.

Additional Ideas/Notes

_____

_____

_____

_____

_____

Directions: Choose a subject from below or one of your own. Follow the directions in the Writer's Notebook (page 68) for writing a cinquain. After writing a rough draft, take your poem through the writing process. Illustrate it if you choose.

Subject Ideas:

- Santa Claus
- your mom
- your cat
- pumpkin
- your friend
- San Francisco
- your dad
- your dog
- television star

Pattern

Title_____

Line 1—One word (noun or name)

Line 2—Two adjectives describing Line 1

Line 3—Three verbs telling what Line 1 does

Line 4—Four words telling more about Line 1

Line 5—Word that means same as Line 1

Lesson 36B—Writing a Haiku

Directions: Choose a subject from nature below or one of your own. Follow the directions in the Writer's Notebook (page 69) for writing a haiku. After writing a rough draft, take your poem through the writing process. Illustrate it if you choose.

Subject Ideas:

- rose
- wind
- parrot
- brook
- volcano
- ocean
- fall leaves
- bee
- forest

Pattern

Title_____

Line 1—five syllables

Line 2—seven syllables

Line 3—five syllables

Lesson 36C—Writing a Tanka

Directions: Choose a subject from nature below or one of your own. Follow the directions in the Writer's Notebook (page 70) for writing a tanka. After writing a rough draft, take your poem through the writing process. Illustrate it if you choose.

Subject Ideas

- sun
- river
- space

- earth
- jungle
- meadow

- stars
- desert
- mountains

Pattern

Title_____

Line 1—five syllables

Line 2—seven syllables

Line 3—five syllables

Line 4—seven syllables

Line 5—seven syllables

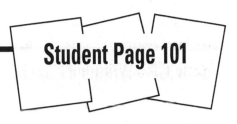

Lesson 36D—Writing a Couplet

Directions: Choose a subject for a couplet from below or one of your own. Follow the directions in the Writer's Notebook (page 71) for writing a couplet. After writing a rough draft, take your poem through the writing process. Illustrate it if you choose.

Subject Ideas:

- insects
- frog
- a holiday
- yourself

- snake
- chimpanzee
- weekends
- your room

- witch
- cobweb
- school
- someone you admire

Pattern

Title_____

Line 1—Begin with descriptive word and add two items that fit description

Line 2—Something that rhymes with Line 1

Lesson 36E—Writing a Limerick

Directions: Choose a subject for a limerick. Keep in mind that limericks are usually humorous. Follow the directions in the Writer's Notebook (page 71) for writing a limerick. After writing a rough draft, take your poem through the writing process. Illustrate it if you choose.

Pattern

Title_____

Line 1—three accented syllables

Line 2—three accented syllables; rhyme with Line 1

Line 3—two accented syllables

Line 4—two accented syllables; rhyme with Line 3

Line 5—three accented syllables; rhyme with Line 1

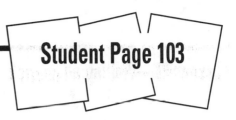

Lesson 36F—Writing an Ode

Directions: Think about someone or something very important to you and write an ode in honor of your choice. Refer to the example in the Writer's Notebook (page 73).

Subject Ideas:

- your pet
- your room
- your computer
- a season you enjoy
- your friend
- your favorite shirt
- a food you like
- your parent or grandparent
- a souvenir or collector's item
- a favorite toy when you were young

_____

_____

_____

_____

_____

_____

_____

_____

_____

_____

_____

_____

_____

_____

_____

_____

_____

There are many ways to publish and share writing. Here are some of them.

- cartoons
- rebus stories
- posters
- bumper stickers
- illustrated storybooks
- book of lists
- dictionary
- dictionary of slang terms
- music lyrics
- pen pal letter exchange
- letters to the editor
- autobiographies
- travel brochures
- trip journals
- postcards
- book reports
- sequels or prequels

- diary of a famous person
- directions
- a day in the life of _____
- letters of complaint
- ads for a new product
- a theater script
- a puppet show script
- reader's theater script
- writing on a kite (and fly it)
- use the computer and print it
- write it on the board
- be videotaped while reading it
- frame it
- write it on a T-shirt
- mail it to a friend
- hang it on a mobile

Additional Ideas/Notes

_____

_____

_____

_____

_____

_____

_____

Turn to the next page for places to publish outside of the classroom.

Teacher's Guide

Here are some places to publish outside of the classroom.

1. **The Perfection Form Company**
   1000 North Second Avenue
   Logan, Iowa 51546

2, **Merlyn's Pen: National Magazine of Student Writing**
   P.O. Box 1058
   98 Main Street
   E. Greenwich, RI 02818-9946

3. **The Flying Pencil Press**
   P.O. Box 7667
   Elgin, IL 60121

4. **Cricket League**
   P.O. Box 300
   Peru, IL 61354

5. **Stone Soup**
   P.O. Box 83
   Santa Cruz, CA 95063

6. **Highlights for Children**
   803 Church Street
   Honesdale, PA 18431

7. **The National Written and Illustrated By . . . Award Contest for Children**
   Landmark Editions, Inc.
   P.O. Box 4469
   Kansas City, MO 64127

Writing Prompts

☐ The best way for students to improve as writers is to write. On the following pages you will find a variety of writing prompts at the head of each page. Distribute them one at a time to the students, allowing them to take each through the writing process.

☐ Use the space below to add your own prompts. A lined page is provided on page 74 of the Writer's Notebook so that you can type in your own idea and then duplicate it for the students.

Additional Ideas/Notes

_____

_____

_____

_____

_____

_____

_____

_____

_____

_____

_____

_____

_____

_____

_____

_____

_____

_____

_____

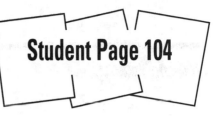

The Day the Babies Ran the World

Directions: Use your imagination to tell a story of when the world's babies take over in power.

_____

_____

_____

_____

_____

_____

_____

_____

_____

_____

_____

_____

_____

_____

_____

_____

_____

_____

_____

_____

_____

_____

_____

The Eighth Dwarf

Directions: Use your imagination to create and tell about the unknown eighth dwarf.

_____

_____

_____

_____

_____

_____

_____

_____

_____

_____

_____

_____

_____

_____

_____

_____

_____

_____

_____

_____

The Wolf and Red-Rising Hood: A Love Story

Directions: Write an alternative for the traditional tale.

_____

_____

_____

_____

_____

_____

_____

_____

_____

_____

_____

_____

_____

_____

_____

_____

_____

_____

_____

_____

_____

_____

_____

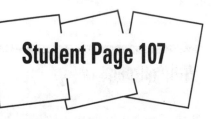

Excuse Me, Rover, Did You Say Something?

Directions: What would happen if your dog could suddenly talk? Write about it here.

_____

_____

_____

_____

_____

_____

_____

_____

_____

_____

_____

_____

_____

_____

_____

_____

_____

_____

_____

_____

_____

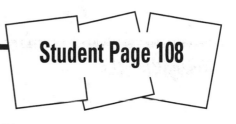
If I Ran the School

Directions: Tell about your day as a school principal if you could do anything you wanted.

_____

_____

_____

_____

_____

_____

_____

_____

_____

_____

_____

_____

_____

_____

_____

_____

_____

_____

_____

_____

_____

What Do You Mean, "The Next Stop Is Mars"?

Directions: Imagine you are on an airplane when suddenly you discover it is headed for Mars. Write a story about your experiences.

_____

_____

_____

_____

_____

_____

_____

_____

_____

_____

_____

_____

_____

_____

_____

_____

_____

_____

_____

_____

_____

_____

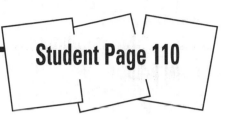
After Happily-Ever-After

Directions: Choose a favorite fairy tale and write what happens after the traditional ending.

_____

_____

_____

_____

_____

_____

_____

_____

_____

_____

_____

_____

_____

_____

_____

_____

_____

_____

_____

_____

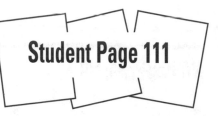

Life Under the City

Directions: Imagine that people live under your city. Describe what life is like there.

_____

_____

_____

_____

_____

_____

_____

_____

_____

_____

_____

_____

_____

_____

_____

_____

_____

_____

_____

_____

_____

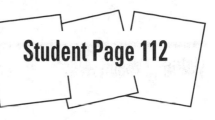

Sherlock Holmes and the Missing Homework

Directions: Write a mystery story involving some missing homework. If you do not know who Sherlock Holmes is, create another detective.

_____

_____

_____

_____

_____

_____

_____

_____

_____

_____

_____

_____

_____

_____

_____

_____

_____

_____

_____

_____

_____

_____

_____

_____

The Day the Sun Forgot to Set

Directions: Imagine a day when the sun does not set. Write a legend about this experience.

_____

_____

_____

_____

_____

_____

_____

_____

_____

_____

_____

_____

_____

_____

_____

_____

_____

_____

_____

_____

_____

_____

_____

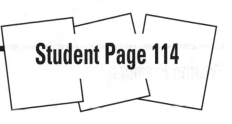

The Day the Ocean Froze

Directions: Imagine a day when the ocean freezes around the world. Write a legend about this experience.

_____

_____

_____

_____

_____

_____

_____

_____

_____

_____

_____

_____

_____

_____

_____

_____

_____

_____

_____

You've Met Batman, Spiderman, and Wonder Woman; Now Meet...

Directions: Create your own superhero, either a serious or a humorous one. Describe him or her in detail.

_____

_____

_____

_____

_____

_____

_____

_____

_____

_____

_____

_____

_____

_____

_____

_____

_____

_____

_____

_____

_____

Part II

✓Writer's Notebook

Writer's Notebook

I. Pre-writing—It precedes writing; the writer activates his thoughts and creativity and writes an outline of these thoughts.

II. Writing First Draft—Develop information from an outline in rough draft form, narrowing pre-writing generalities to specifics.

III. Responding—(optional) Allow someone else to interpret what one has written and offer suggestions.

IV. Revising—The writer changes and improves his works by reworking a sentence/paragraph with consideration for organization, clarity, unity, emphasis, and word selection.

V. Editing—This is similar to revising, including sentence combining and use of editing checklist.

VI. Recopying—Make a new copy of revised, edited work.

VII. Final proofreading—Make a final, careful check for spelling, punctuation, etc.

VIII. Follow-up illustrations

On each of the Parts-of-Speech pages, write a running list of words that fit each category. Use additional pages, as necessary.

Nouns	Pronouns
words that name a person, place, thing, or idea	words used in place of a noun

Writer's Notebook

Verbs

words that show action or a state of being (existence)

Adjectives

words that describe a noun or pronoun

Adverbs

words that modify a verb, adjective, or other adverb

Prepositions

words that show how the object and another word are related

Writer's Notebook

Conjunctions

words that connect other words

Interjections

words used to show strong emotion

Diagramming Sentences

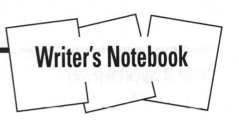

Here are basic diagram forms for sentences.

1. | subject | verb |

2. | noun |
    \adjective

3. | verb |
    \adverb

4. | word modified |
    \preposition
      | object |

5. | subject | verb | direct object |

6. | subject | verb \ subject complement |

a. I am happy today.

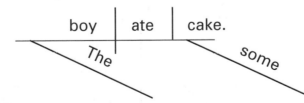

b. The boy ate some cake.

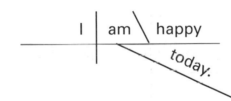

c. Under the bridge sat the spotted frog.

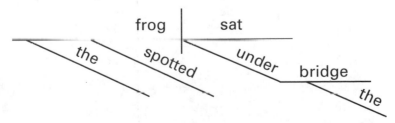

Conjugating Verbs

To *conjugate* a verb means to write it in each of its six tenses. A tense of a verb shows the time frame in which it takes place.

The six tenses are these:
- **present tense**—happening now or regularly
- **past tense**—happened at a particular time in the past
- **future tense**—will happen
- **present perfect tense**—began in the past and continues or is completed now
- **past perfect tense**—began and was completed in the past
- **future perfect tense**—will begin and be completed in the future

Example of the conjugation of a regular verb (to paint) in the first person singular (I):
> I paint. (present)
> I painted. (past)
> I will paint. (future)
> I have painted. (present perfect)
> I had painted. (past perfect)
> I will have painted. (future perfect)

Example of the conjugation of an irregular verb (to draw) in the first person singular (I):
> I draw. (present)
> I drew. (past)
> I will draw. (future)
> I have drawn. (present perfect)
> I had drawn. (past perfect)
> I will have drawn. (future perfect)

Chart of the principle conjugation parts of 40 irregular verbs:

present	past	past participle	present	past	past participle
am/be	was/were	been	lie (recline)	lay	lain
begin	began	begun	ride	rode	ridden
bite	bit	bitten	ring	rang	rung
blow	blew	blown	rise	rose	risen
break	broke	broken	run	ran	run
bring	brought	brought	see	saw	seen
catch	caught	caught	shake	shook	shaken
come	came	come	shine (light)	shone	shone
do	did	done	shrink	shrank	shrunk
drink	drank	drunk	sing	sang/sung	sung
drive	drove	driven	sit	sat	sat
drown	drowned	drowned	speak	spoke	spoken
eat	ate	eaten	steal	stole	stolen
fly	flew	flown	swim	swam	swum
give	gave	given	swing	swung	swung
go	went	gone	take	took	taken
grow	grew	grown	tear	tore	torn
hide	hid	hidden/hid	throw	threw	thrown
know	knew	known	wake	woke/waked	waked
lay	laid	laid	wear	wore	worn

Sensory Words for Describing Food

Shape	Taste	Texture	Odor
indiscriminate	biting	cold	delicious
oblong	bittersweet	dry	fishy
oval	bland	gooey	fresh
round	burnt	grainy	meaty
square	buttery	gritty	pungent
tapered	creamy	hard	salty
	crisp	hot	savory
	delicious	icy	smoky
	fishy	moist	sour
	flavorful	oily	spicy
	fruity	rough	strong
	gingery	slimy	sweet
	grainy	smooth	
	hearty	soft	
	hot	sticky	
	juicy	waxy	
	mild		
	minty		
	nutty		
	oily		
	peppery		
	salty		
	savory		
	smooth		
	sour		
	spicy		
	strong		
	sugary		
	sweet		
	tangy		
	tart		
	tasteless		
	tasty		
	vinegar		

Sensory Words for Describing Objects

Size/Weight	**Shape**	**Texture**		**Sound**
bulky	broad	bumpy	gooey	thumping
colossal	crooked	crinkled	gritty	squeaking
enormous	curved	fluffy	dull	tinkling
gigantic	deep	muddy	furry	ringing
huge	shallow	murky	greasy	clanging
tiny	square	rippling	earthy	sizzling
immense	round	shear	lukewarm	screeching
huge	oblong	wispy	rubbery	hissing
massive	tapered	cold	tepid	humming
minute	many sided	icy	slushy	rustling
towering	indiscriminate	hot		buzzing
light		warm		popping
	Color	smooth		splashing
	flaming	rough		thudding
	dart	grainy		snapping
	bright	sandy		
	glowing	moist		**Odor**
	flashing	dry		antiseptic
	dull	satiny		burning
	pale	silky		clean
	flickering	velvety		fresh
	glaring	oily		fragrant
	dazzling	slippery		medicinal
	radiant	uneven		musty
	colorful	jogged		pungent
	shiny	prickly		putrid
	multicolored	hairy		strong
		shaggy		sweet
		cool		
		cuddly		
		elastic		
		tickly		
		moist		
		damp		
		downy		
		hard		
		slimy		
		sharp		
		stick		
		soft		
		solid		
		sticky		
		wet		

Sensory Words for Describing Animals and People

Eyes

beady
black
blue
bright
brilliant
brown
clear
dark
dazzling
dreamy
dull
enormous
expressive
flashing
flaming
glaring
gleaming
glistening
glowing
gray
large
laughing
oval
radiant
shimmering
sparkling
starry
wide

Ears

droopy
floppy
huge
pointed
rounded
small

Stature/Body Build

bent
big
bulky
chubby
colossal
crooked
enormous
fat
gigantic
graceful
grotesque
heavy
huge
immense
large
light
little
long
massive
minute
petite
portly
short
skinny
small
stout
tall
thin
tiny
towering

Tail

flat
long
short
stubby
thin

Hair/Body Covering

bald
black
blonde
brown
brunette
coarse
crinkled
curly
dark
feathered
fluffy
fuzzy
glistening
golden
green
gray
long
multicolored
red
scaly
short
smooth
spotted
straight
thick
white
yellow

Complexion

black
blushing
dark
light
pale
radiant
rosy
ruddy
tan
white
wizened
wrinkled

Sounds

bark
bawl
bleat
cackle
coo
crook
cry
groan
growl
hoot
howl
hiss
peep
purr
scream
screech
snarl
snort
squared
tweet
wail
whine

Personality

bold
ferocious
fierce
generous
gentle
happy
kingly
mean
shy
vicious

Weather

balmy
breezy
cold
cool
damp
dusty
dry
foggy
frosty
hazy
hot
humid
murky
rainy
starry
steamy
stormy
sunny
warm
wet
windy

Sounds

babbling
banging
bellowing
blaring
blasting
booming
bumping
buzzing
cheering
chiming
clamoring
clanging
clapping
clashing
crackling
crashing
crunching
deafening
echoing
exploding
gurgling
hissing
howling
humming
inaudible
jingling
jangling
lapping
loud
noisy
patter
peal
popping
quiet
raging
raspy
raucous
reverberating
ringing
roaring
rowdy
rumbling
rustling

screeching
shrill
silence
sizzling
sloshing
snapping
splashing
squeaking
still
swishing
thud
thumping
thundering
tinkling
tolling
uproar
whimpering
whispering
whistling
working
yelling
zinging

Odors

antiseptic
burning
clean
earthy
fragrant
fresh
gaseous
medicinal
moldy
musty
piney
pungent
rotten
smoky
stagnant
stale
strong
sweet

glad	amused	comfortable	enthralled
peaceful	thrilled	joyful	delighted
cheerful	proud	excited	ecstatic
satisfied	pleased	contented	courageous

Happiness or Pleasure

unhappy	lonely	tearful	nervous
disappointed	gloomy	upset	frightened
discouraged	sorrowful	troubled	fearful
hopeless	angry	miserable	anxious
pathetic	serious		

Sadness or Apprehension

silly	loony	funny	jovial
comical	jolly	ridiculous	hilarious

Amusement

liking	kind	helpful	true
friendly	generous	fond	pleasant

Loving and Caring

Sequential Words

additionally	immediately
after	in addition
afterward	in the first place
always	last
another	later
as soon as	more
at last	next
at once	now
at the same time	on time
before	second
beforehand	since
during	subsequently
earlier	then
(a) few	thereafter
finally	third
first	until
further	when
furthermore	while

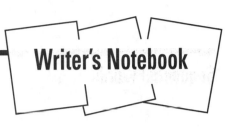

I. To add or emphasize an idea

above	further	similarly
again	furthermore	
also	in addition	
equally important	moreover	

II. To indicate contrast between ideas

although	notwithstanding	though
beside	on the contrary	yet
different than	on the other hand	
however	otherwise	
instead of	rather than	
nevertheless	still	

III. To explain or illustrate an idea

as though	for instance
for example	such as

IV. To show result or consequence

accordingly	due	so that
as	hence	therefore
as a result	in fact	thus
because	just as	unfortunately
consequently	so	

V. To summarize

in short

in summary

to conclude

VI. To show ideas are similar

similarly

likewise

Synonyms

about—concerning, regarding, relating to, referring to dealing with

almost—about, nearly

ask—question, request, inquire

awkward—clumsy, bungling, inept, rough

add—join, unite, accompany, associate, combine

accomplish—do, achieve, attain, fulfill

attractive—lovely, beautiful, captivating

charming—delightful, elegant, enchanting

ability—power, capability, energy, force, might

automobile—car, vehicle

alarm—surprise, astound, amaze, astonish, bewilder, startle

advise—teach, direct, educate, inform, train, tutor, suggest

apply—utilize, use, employ, operate

ache—pain, affliction, agony, distress, misery

bored—tired, exhausted, fatigued

beneath—under, below, underneath

bad—naughty, evil, wicked, villainous

begin—start, commence, originate

before—prior to, previous, prior

big—large, enormous, gigantic, great, huge, mighty

boy—lad, guy, youth, fellow, youngster

bold—valiant, brave, courageous, daring, fearless, heroic

brilliant—bright, clear, gleaming, radiant, shimmering

build—construct, erect, make, put up, manufacture

bare—empty, vacant, barren, cold

battle—fight, encounter, brawl, contest, encounter, quarrel

creek—brook, stream, rivulet

call—summon, command, cry, address, demand, exclaim, proclaim, shout

capture—apprehend, catch, take, trap

Writer's Notebook

carry—bring, lug, transport, convey, support

comfort—ease, assist, console, encourage

completion—finish, finale, conclusion, termination

companion—friend, buddy, pal, ally, comrade

colossal—huge, vast, enormous, immense, gigantic, tremendous

calm—mild, gentle, mellow, soothing, placid, cool, peaceful, quiet, serene

certain—sure, unquestionable, inevitable, undeniable, definite

children—youngsters, juveniles

crowd—push, shove, force, jostle

correct—right, honest, just, accurate, valid, proper

change—alter, substitute, modify, vary, transform

conclusion—end, finish, conclusion, completion, termination

conceited—vain, empty, frivolous, hollow

close—shut, seal

caring—kind, gentle, benevolent, amiable, loving

devour—eat, consume, gobble

develop—grow, mature, develop, expand, increase

delicious—tasty, flavorful, zestful, savory

disregard—ignore, pass over, take no account of

durable—hard, rigid, compact, firm, solid, strong, difficult

during—while, simultaneously

demonstrate—show, display, exhibit

enough—sufficient, adequate, ample, plenty

error—mistake, blunder, failure, fault, misconception, oversight

empire—nation, country, community, realm, kingdom

evil—wicked, corrupt, vile

frequently—often, generally, repeatedly, oftentimes

find—discover, uncover, come across, run across, stumble up

food—nourishment, sustenance

fragment—part, portion, allotment, bit, piece, scrap

fast—quick, rapid, brisk, hasty, swift

firm—tough, hardy, strong, sturdy

give—grant, provide, furnish, present, supply

good—suitable, honest, reliable, worthy, righteous

got—became

grand—great, huge, enormous, large, vast

glen—valley

globe—world, earth

have—possess, control, obtain, own

help—assist, aid, encourage, facilitate

idea—concept, belief, impression, opinion, thought

keep on—resume, continue

know—realize, understand, comprehend

learn—understand, acquire, determine, ascertain

last—final, end

let—allow, permit, tolerate

like—comparable, equal, related

long—extended, lengthy, lasting, prolonged

look—appear to, seem

neat—orderly, clear, exact, precise, spotless, tidy

new—recent, fresh, strange, unfamiliar, untried

now—presently, currently

next—after, following, proceeding

ocean—sea

old—aged, ancient, antique, elderly, obsolete

play—romp, skip, frolic, perform, imagine

picture—design, drawing, facsimile, illustration, likeness, photo, portrait

plan—devise, invent, map, prepare

put—set, deposit, install, place

reply—answer, respond, acknowledge

right—correct

stupid—dumb, brainless, dense, dull, senseless

stretchable—elastic, flexible, pliable

small—little, elfin, petite, slight, tiny, wee

spot—place, abode, home, area, locality, regime

say—state, affirm, allege, assert, declare, express

slender—thin, gaunt, slim

stop—halt, cease, interrupt, hinder

story—fable, tale, legend, fantasy

strange—rare, unusual, unknown, uncommon

strong—sturdy, athletic, durable, enduring, solid, tough

study—examine, investigate, scrutinize, contemplate

tall—lofty, high, elevated, towering

top—summit, peak, crest, cap, pinnacle

tell—relate, describe, narrate, notify, report, declare, express, say, speak, reveal

think—imagine, consider, picture, contemplate, determine, reflect, suppose, believe

trapped—cornered, captured, seduced

troubled—worried, anxious, apprehensive

time—period, date, era, season

try—endeavor, attempt

use—utilize, apply, employ, operate

very—greatly, enormously, extremely, immensely, intensely, unusually, immeasurably, exceedingly, truly, infinitely, incredibly, fully, mightily, especially

walking—strolling, wandering

want—desire, aspire, covet, crave, long for, wish

weird—strange, unusual, unique

work—labor, accomplishment, action, achievement, task, job, profession

worry—anxiety, apprehension, concern, troubled

write—record, compose, correspond, draft, scribble

zero—nothing, blank, naught, nil, nonentity

Common Synonyms and Related Words

(See page 35 for synonyms for *said*.)

Go	Make	Do
arrive	blend	bring
chase	build	buy
crawl	carve	capture
enter	color	carry
fall	copy	collect
float	cut	cover
fly	draw	discover
glide	fix	earn
hop	form	end
jump	mix	escape
leap	mold	fill
leave	pour	frighten
plunge	repair	hide
ride	stir	hold
run	stuff	know
skip	tear	lead
slide		left
soar		lose
spin		move
travel		open
tumble		own
twirl		pick
walk		play
		quit
		reach
		receive
		remove
		seize
		shave
		shop
		start
		steer
		strike
		sew
		teach
		trick
		win
		work

Homonyms

A *homonym* is a word that sounds the same as another word but has a different meaning. Add the homonyms you find from Student Page 37. One has been done for you.

ate – **eight**

_____ – _____   _____ – _____

_____ – _____   _____ – _____

_____ – _____   _____ – _____

_____ – _____   _____ – _____

_____ – _____   _____ – _____

_____ – _____   _____ – _____

_____ – _____   _____ – _____

_____ – _____   _____ – _____

_____ – _____   _____ – _____

_____ – _____   _____ – _____

_____ – _____   _____ – _____

_____ – _____   _____ – _____

_____ – _____   _____ – _____

_____ – _____   _____ – _____

_____ – _____   _____ – _____

_____ – _____   _____ – _____

_____ – _____   _____ – _____

Antonyms

An *antonym* is a word with the opposite meaning of another word. Add to the list below the antonyms you find from Student Page 39. One has been done for you.

answer – ask

_____ – _____   _____ – _____

_____ – _____   _____ – _____

_____ – _____   _____ – _____

_____ – _____   _____ – _____

_____ – _____   _____ – _____

_____ – _____   _____ – _____

_____ – _____   _____ – _____

_____ – _____   _____ – _____

_____ – _____   _____ – _____

_____ – _____   _____ – _____

_____ – _____   _____ – _____

_____ – _____   _____ – _____

_____ – _____   _____ – _____

_____ – _____   _____ – _____

_____ – _____   _____ – _____

_____ – _____   _____ – _____

_____ – _____

Similes

A *simile* is a phrase that compares two unlike things in order to describe one of them, using the word *like* or *as.* Add to the list below the similes you find from Student Page 43.

blind as a bat	playful as a kitten
brave as a lion	pleased as punch
brown as a berry	pretty as a picture
cheap as dirt	proud as a peacock
clean as a whistle	quick as a wink
cold as ice	right as rain
crazy as a loon	round as a ball
deaf as a post	sharp as a tack
dumb as an ox	shy as a violet
easy as pie	sick as a dog
fat as a hog	sly as a fox
fit as a fiddle	smart as a whip
flat as a flounder	stubborn as a mule
free as a breeze	straight as an arrow
gentle as a lamb	strong as an ox
good as gold	sweet as sugar
green as grass	thin as a rail
hard as nails	ugly as sin
light as a feather	warm as toast
neat as a pin	white as a sheet
nervous as a cat	wrinkled as a prune

Metaphors

A *metaphor* is a phrase that compares two unlike things. While a simile **compares** two things that are unlike by using the words *as* or *like*, a metaphor **states that one thing is** the other. Add to the list below the metaphors you find from Student Page 45.

Books are food for the brain.

An eye is the window to the world.

A flower is a bee's dining room.

Youth is the prelude to maturity.

The ocean is a huge swimming pool.

Life is the world's gift to man.

Winter is the hibernation of the earth.

Earth is the mother of mankind.

_____   _____

_____

_____

_____

_____

_____

_____

_____

_____

_____

_____

_____

_____

Idioms

An *idiom* is an expression which means something different from what is actually said. For example, "to put one's foot in one's mouth" does not literally mean to place one's foot inside one's mouth! This expression means "to say something one should not have said."

Here are some common idioms and their meanings. As you think of more, add them to this list:

Idioms	**Meanings**
turn over a new leaf	begin again
spill the beans	tell a secret
hold your horses	wait
to be downhearted	to be sad
hit the ceiling	become angry
hold your tongue	be quiet
see eye to eye	agree
in a pickle	having a hard time
for the birds	silly or useless
a close shave	a close encounter with trouble
put on the dog	try to be extra fancy
going to the dogs	falling apart
in one ear and out the other	you hear but do not pay attention
crocodile tears	fake tears
raining cats and dogs	raining heavily
_____	_____
_____	_____
_____	_____
_____	_____

Alliteration

Alliteration is the repetition of the beginning sound of two or more words in a sentence to emphasize a description or point. Add your alliterative phrases and sentences from Student Page 49 to the list below. Add others as you think of them.

- A busy bumble bee buzzed boldly toward us.

- The wicked, wild witch walked with her wobbly cane down to the watchtower.

- A cute, cuddly cat capered through the cattails.

- A sleek, streamlined spaceship sped through the stars.

- A raucous, red rooster crowed from the rooftops.

- A slim silhouette sauntered down the sidewalk.

- A brilliantly beautiful bluebird sat upon a branch.

_____

_____

_____

_____

_____

_____

_____

_____

_____

_____

_____

_____

_____

_____

Hyperbole

Here are some examples of *hyperbole,* exaggerated statements to make a point. Add other examples of hyperbole to this list.

- I was so tired I could have slept for a year.

- When she saw the bear, the girl became glued to the ground.

- I could have danced all night.

- The man was so cold he turned blue.

- I ate so much I almost burst.

- He talked until he was blue in the face.

- The tree was so tall it reached the sky.

- Mary choked on her own laughter.

- The swing took her halfway to heaven.

- The class was so noisy, you could not hear yourself think.

_____

_____

_____

_____

_____

_____

_____

_____

_____

_____

_____

_____

Using Personification

Personification is the technique of giving animate qualities to inanimate objects. Review the examples of personification below. Add others of your own to the list.

- The sound of the gong announced dinner was being served.

- The chair tumbled over.

- The pine tree reached its leafy arms skyward.

- The paper flew off the table.

- The house stood on dry land.

- The raindrops danced on the windowpane.

- Perspiration rolled down her back.

- The book sat on the desk.

- The floor groaned as the dancers leaped upon it.

- The wind whispered through the trees.

- The leaves danced in the wind.

_____

_____

_____

_____

_____

_____

_____

_____

_____

_____

_____

Unusual Word Combinations

Unusual descriptive word combinations in writing are similar to metaphors in that unlike things are often compared in order to create emphasis. They are also sometimes like *oxymorons* in that two things are combined that should be mutually exclusive. Regardless of the form they take, the result of the word combinations is an unusual description that captures the reader's attention and imagination, painting a vivid picture for the reader to envision.

To the page below, add unusual word combination sentences from Student Pages 55–57, as well as any others you would like to record. Two examples have been given.

- A raging storm at sea brightened a tropical island.
- The first rays of sunlight kissed the mountain top.

_____

_____

_____

_____

_____

_____

_____

_____

_____

_____

_____

_____

_____

_____

_____

_____

To expand a basic sentence:

1. Add two adjectives.

2. Add how (adverb).

3. Add where (prepositional phrase).

4. Add when (prepositional phrase).

5. Add why.

6. Use a simile or metaphor, if possible.

7. Use alliteration, if possible.

8. Use personifications, if possible.

9. Use hyperbole, if possible.

10. Use as many synonyms as possible for given words.

Ways to Begin a Sentence

There are many ways to begin a sentence. Here are some of the best.

Sentence: The ballerinas dance.

1. **Two adjectives**

   Example: Lovely, graceful ballerinas dance.

   or

   Lovely and graceful ballerinas dance.

2. **A question**

   Example: Who are those lovely, graceful ballerinas dancing across the floor?

3. **A prepositional phrase**

   Example: In the spotlight, the lovely, graceful ballerinas dance.

Prepositions

about	beneath	inside	throughout
above	beside	into	to
across	between	near	toward
after	beyond	of	under
against	by	off	until
along	concerning	on	up
among	down	out	upon
around	during	over	with
at	except	past	within
before	for	regarding	without
behind	from	since	
below	in	through	

4. **Infinitive Verb** ("to" plus verb)

   Example: To dance at night before a receptive audience is a pleasure for the ballerinas.

5. **Gerund Verb** (verb plus "ing")

   Example: Smiling at the vast audience, the ballerinas dance.

6. **Interjection**

   Example: Amazing! The ballerinas are unbelievably graceful.

Sentence Starters

The following words are useful for beginning sentences. Add others you know to the list.

- after
- although
- as
- before
- beyond
- during
- finally
- if
- in spite of
- instead of
- last night
- on the way to
- rather than
- since
- suddenly
- this afternoon (morning, evening)
- yesterday
- when
- while

How to Construct a Paragraph

When writing a paragraph, it is a good idea to think of its complete structure. In general, a paragraph should have a **topic sentence**, **approximately three support sentences**, and a **conclusion**. It is all right to write paragraphs in other ways, too, but if you know this way, you will be able to write any paragraph better.

1. Choose a topic.

2. Write a topic sentence to introduce the subject of the paragraph.

3. Provide supporting details about the subject, each in its own sentence. There should be at least three supporting sentences.

4. Write a concluding sentence. It may be like one of the following:

   - the topic sentence repeated

   - the topic sentence written in a different way

   - a sentence stating the results of the preceding sentences

   - an exclamation summarizing the emotion of the previous sentences

   - the desired results emanating from the previous sentences

   - a personal opinion based upon the preceding sentences

5. Optional: Write an appropriate title.

In order to use quotation marks in your writing, you will need to follow these guidelines.

---

1. Enclose the words each speaker says in quotation marks.

2. Start a new paragraph each time a different speaker begins to speak.

3. Conclude the actual words of a speaker with a comma, question mark, or exclamation point placed before the concluding quotation mark. If the end of the speaker's words come at the close of a sentence, conclude with end punctuation (period, exclamation point, or question mark) and then close quotes.

4. In general, it is a good idea to use *said* or a synonym of *said* and the name of the speaker either before or after the quote.

Examples:

Tom asked, "Can Jim and I go to the mall to buy some new shoes?"

"Have you cleaned your room yet?" questioned Mom.

"No," answered Tom.

Mom replied, "Room first, and then the mall."

"All right," grumbled Tom.

Synonyms for *Said*

acknowledged	decided	murmured	screamed
added	demanded	nagged	shouted
admitted	denied	noted	shrieked
advised	described	notified	snapped
agreed	dictated	objected	sneered
announced	emphasized	observed	sobbed
answered	estimated	ordered	spoke
approved	exclaimed	pleaded	sputtered
argued	explained	pointed out	stammered
assumed	expressed	prayed	stated
assured	feared	predicted	stormed
asked	giggled	questioned	suggested
babbled	grinned	reassured	taunted
bargained	grunted	related	thought
began	indicated	repeated	told
boasted	insisted	replied	urged
bragged	instructed	responded	uttered
called	laughed	requested	vowed
claimed	lectured	restated	wailed
commanded	lied	revealed	warned
commented	mentioned	roared	whispered
complained	moaned	ruled	
cried	mumbled	scolded	

Writer's Notebook

OPENING

- Have an exciting opening sentence.
- Set the scene.
- Present main characters.
- Introduce the problem.

END

- Briefly describe how all parts of the story come together in a satisfactory solution.

MIDDLE

- Introduce secondary characters.
- Elaborate on the problem.
- Show attempts made to solve the problem.
- Show logical action leading to the climax.

CLIMAX

- This is the most exciting part. It must show the process for solution of the problem.

Scene and Setting Outline

Use this outline form to help you plan for writing a story.

Time

Place

Weather

Sounds

Smells (if any)

Sights

    People

    Animals (if any)

    Plants (if any)

Other Important Information

Special Vocabulary

Describing Characters

Main Character(s)

Name	**Name**
Physical Description	Physical Description
Age (young, old, middle-aged)	Age (young, old, middle-aged)
Hair (color, length, style)	Hair (color, length, style)
Complexion (fair, dark)	Complexion (fair, dark)
Stature (tall, short, husky, slim)	Stature (tall, short, husky, slim)
Eyes (color, size, shape, expression)	Eyes (color, size, shape, expression)
Personality	Personality
Talents	Talents
Emotional state	Emotional state
Motivation	Motivation
Clothing	Clothing

Story Outline

Use this and the following sheets to help you prepare and organize your story.

I. Opening

Provide an exciting beginning, a question, exclamation, or description. Briefly describe the main characters, placing them at an important scene or setting. Present the problem(s) that the story will handle.

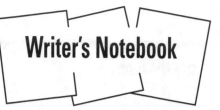

II. Middle

Show interaction of the characters.

Explain the problem(s) in greater detail.

Describe how the characters are trying to solve the problem(s).

Build up to the climax.

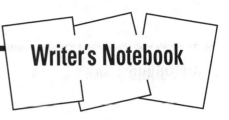

III. Climax

Show the characters solving the problem(s) or reaching the turning point from which the problem will be solved.

IV. Denouement (conclusion)

Explain what the characters have learned.

Tie up all loose ends.

Provide a brief ending.

Dead Words

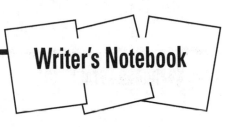

Some words in the English language tend to be overused and therefore lose their power. These are called *dead words*. Below is a list of dead words and more interesting alternatives. Add others to the list on a continuing basis.

also—too, moreover, besides, as well as, in addition to

awesome, cool, rad—fine, wonderful, marvelous, great, fantastic, marvelous

scared—afraid, fearful, terrified, frightened

have to—need to, must

very—extremely, exceedingly, fantastically, unusually, incredibly, intensely, truly, fully, especially, shockingly, bitterly, immeasurably, infinitely, severely, surely, mightily, powerfully, chiefly

like—such as, similar to, similarly

kid—child, boy, girl, youngster, youth

mad—angry, frustrated, furious, incensed, enraged

got, get—received, obtained, attained, succeed in

then—first, second, next, later, finally, afterward, meanwhile, soon

nice—pleasant, charming, fascinating, captivating, delightful, pleasurable, pleasing

lots—numerous, heaps, many, scores, innumerable

so—thus, accordingly, therefore

fun—pleasant, pleasurable, amusing, entertaining, jolly

good—excellent, exceptional, fine, marvelous, splendid, superb, wonderful

but—however, moreover, yet, still, nevertheless, though, although, on the other hand

awful—dreadful, alarming, frightful, terrible, horrid, shocking

great—wonderful, marvelous, fantastic

guy—man, person, fellow, boy

funny—amusing, comical, laughable, jovial

Your name:_____

Author's name: _____

Mark an "x" under the appropriate place on the provided lines:

	very much	somewhat
1. I enjoyed reading this.		
2. This made sense to me.		
3. The writing is imaginative.		

Finish the following statements as best you can. Remember, your job is to help the writer.

1. One thing I really like about this writing is . . .

2. One thing I think the author can improve upon is . . .

3. Something I would like the author to tell more about is . . .

4. One last comment is . . .

Writer's Notebook

Your name:_____

Author's name: _____

I. Check the correct box after you have proofread* for the following. (Write your proofreading marks on the author's paper.)

❑ 1. Capitalization

❑ 2. Punctuation end-marks

❑ 3. Sentence run-ons and fragments

❑ 4. Commas

❑ 5. Quotation marks

❑ 6. New paragraph indentations

❑ 7. Correct spelling

❑ 8. Logic (Makes sense)

II. Something I might change in this writing is . . .

III. Something I would definitely keep in this writing is . . .

*A set of proofreading marks is provided on page 66 of the Writer's Notebook.

Date _____

Dear _____,

Greeting

_____

_____

_____

_____

_____

_____

_____

_____

_____

_____

_____

_____

_____

_____

_____

_____

Closing: Love/Affectionately/Fondly,

_____

Signature

Form for Addressing an Envelope

Stamp

Name (Sender)
Address (Number and Street)
City, State and Zip

Name (Recipient)
Address (Number and Street)
City, State and Zip

Form for a Business Letter

_____

Sender's street number and name

_____

Sender's city, state and zip

_____

Date

_____

Recipient's name

_____

Recipient's number and street name

_____

Recipient's city, state and zip

Dear Sir/Madam:

_____

_____

_____

_____

_____

_____

_____

_____

_____

Closing: Yours truly/sincerely,

_____

Signature

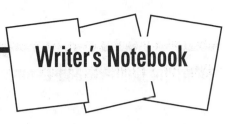
Writer's Notebook

Topic: _____

List Good Points or Likenesses (and examples)	List Bad Points or Differences (and examples)

Writer's Notebook

Topic: _____

Paragraph 1: Tell the good points or likenesses, including examples.

Paragraph 2: Tell the bad points or differences, including examples.

Paragraph 3: Briefly summarize paragraphs 1 and 2.

Writer's Notebook

Topic: _____

Paragraph 1: Describe the incident (the cause). Be sure to state specifically what happens.

Paragraph 2: Describe the result or results of the cause, clearly stating each one. If the results are very different, you may need more than one paragraph to do this.

Paragraph 3: Suggest a remedy to the effects, if they are negative.

Writer's Notebook

Topic: _____

Paragraph 1: Describe what occurred or is occurring.

Paragraph 2: Present the first point of view.

Paragraph 3: Present the second point of view.

Additional paragraphs: Present other points of view, as necessary.

Last paragraph: Present the commonalities.

Topic: _____

Paragraph 1: Give a detailed description of the issue or problem.

Paragraph 2: State why this issue or problem is important to consider.

Paragraph 3: Present the best solution, in your opinion.

Paragraph 4: Write the benefits of the change that will be brought about by your solution.

Writing a Summary

Summaries are brief retellings of a piece of writing. They include only the highlights and important facts. For example, if summarizing the *Tale of Peter Rabbit,* it would only be important to include the facts that Peter was a mischievous rabbit who got into trouble in a farmer's garden because he did not listen to his mother. An expanded summary would include the things he did wrong and the results of his actions.

When writing a summary, read the article or story carefully. Take note of all important facts. Then do the following:

1. List the important facts in your own words.

2. Combine any facts possible.

3. Rewrite the facts as briefly as possible.

_____

_____

_____

_____

_____

_____

_____

_____

_____

_____

_____

_____

_____

_____

_____

_____

_____

Form for Conducting an Interview

Here is a sample outline for questioning an individual concerning his career.

1. Person's whole name

2. Occupation or profession

3. Place of work

4. Length of tenure

5. How did you become interested in this occupation/profession?

6. What are your responsibilities?

7. What part of your work do you like? Why?

8. What part of your work do you dislike? Why?

9. How much and what type of training and/or school was required for your job?

10. Do you think this will be your occupation for the rest of your life? Why or why not?

Writing Results of an Interview

Person's name: _____

Paragraph 1: Choose a good topic sentence that summarizes the focus of your interview. Include the initial information of the interview (items 1–4 on the previous sheet).

Paragraphs 2+: Relate the information from the questions of substance. Each bit of information may need to be a separate paragraph. Determine the information that belongs together.

Final Paragraph: Recap the primary interview information.

General Interview Topics

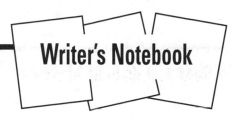

- name
- age
- birth date
- birthplace
- current residence (general)
- family of origin
- family's cultural background
- current family
- friends
- education
- work experience
- current occupation
- job description
- work environment
- interests
- pastimes
- concerns/causes (illiteracy, civil rights, family values, etc.)
- favorites (book, show, color, flower, movie, season, etc.)
- dislikes
- pet peeves
- childhood memories
- beliefs

Outline I for Writing a Newspaper Article

Headline

Byline

Dateline

Illustration (optional)

Paragraph 1: who, what, and where

Paragraph 2+: how and why, organized logically

Last Paragraph: conclusion, summary, or future prospects

List of Headlines

Writer's Notebook

Headline

Byline:	Dateline:

Details

where?	what?

who?	why?

how?

Writing a Book Report

Important things to include in a book report:

Paragraph 1: title, author, illustrator, copyright, and genre (fiction, nonfiction, mystery, biography, etc.)

Paragraph 2: main characters, names, appearances, and how they act

Paragraph 3: time period and setting

Paragraph 4: brief discussion of plot and theme or main idea

Paragraph 5: personal opinion and recommendation

There are many ways to present a book report. Ideas include the following:

Outline

Title

I. _____

   Main topic (Begin each entry with a capital letter.)

   A. _____

      Subtopic (Begin each entry with a capital letter.)

      1. _____

         _____

         _____

         _____

      2. _____

         _____

         _____

         _____

   B. _____

      1. _____

         _____

         _____

         _____

      2. _____

         _____

         _____

         _____

      3. _____

         _____

         _____

         _____

Writer's Notebook

II. _____

    A. _____

        1. _____

        2. _____

        3. _____

        4. _____

    B. _____

        1. _____

        2. _____

        3. _____

        4. _____

III. _____

    A. _____

        1. _____

        2. _____

        3. _____

        4. _____

    B. _____

        1. _____

        2. _____

        3. _____

        4. _____

Web Form

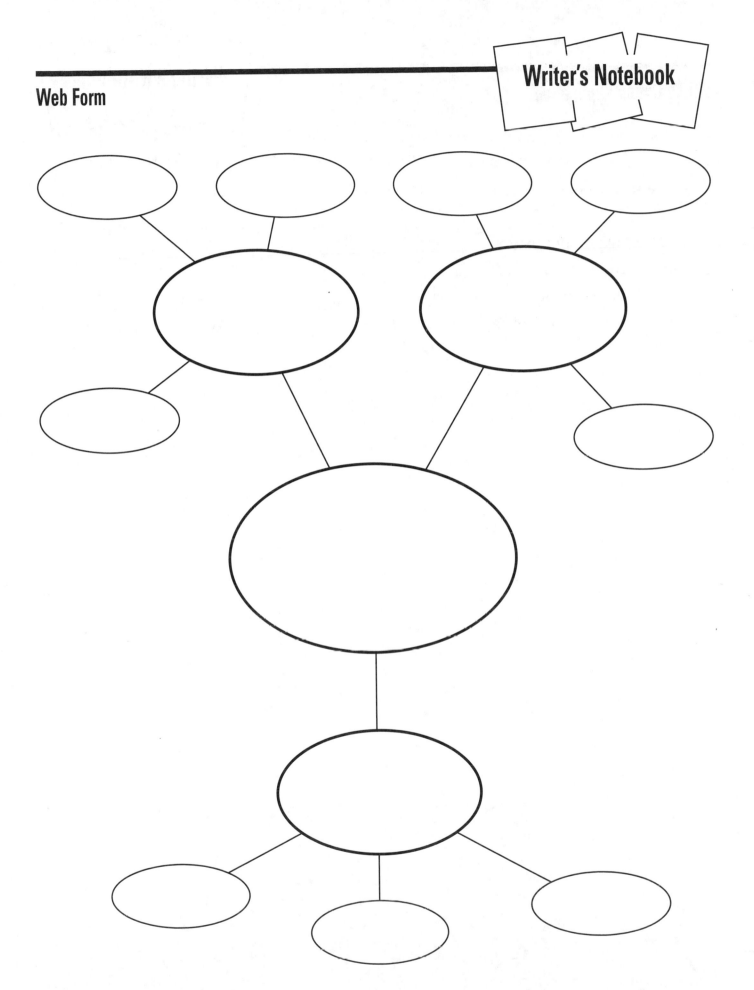

Filling Out an Application

When filling out an application, remember that all of the following matter:

- neatness and legibility
- spelling
- accuracy and honesty
- completion
- information included

If any question on an application does not apply to you, write N/A. This stands for "not applicable."

Following is the information it is usually worthwhile to include on a resumé.

Name

Street Number and Name

City, State, and Zip

Phone Number

Job Objectives

- Why do you want the job?
- What duties will you perform?
- What extra things will you do beyond required duties?
- Why do you think you are right for the job?

Personal Information

- Personal qualifications (reliable, responsible, hardworking, dedicated, conscientious, dependable, trustworthy, etc.); explain briefly the ones chosen

Educational Background

- Schools attended and years of attendance
- Subjects in which you excelled, favorite subject, and extra-curricular activities

Work Experience

- Jobs you have done related to the job for which you are applying

References

- Names and phone numbers of people who can give you a good recommendation

Proofreading Symbols

⋁⋀	insert (put in)
ℛℯ	delete (take out)
Ḉ	capitalize
A̸	lower case
(righte)	misspelled
⋁⋁	wrong word
?	does not make sense
‿	join these words or letters
⸜ₒ	missing word
⁋	new paragraph
N.C.S.	not a complete sentence
D.W.	dead word
⊙	add period
⋀,	add comma
↻→	trade position
⁇⋁	add quotations
#	space

☐ Important words of title are capitalized.

☐ Paragraphs are indented and margins are correct.

☐ Punctuation is correct.

☐ Each sentence is a complete thought.

☐ Most sentences in a paragraph begin with a different word.

☐ Colorful speech (similes, idioms, metaphors, synonyms, personification) is used.

☐ Relative pronouns (who, where, whose, which, that) are used correctly.

☐ Transition words (although, because, when, while, therefore) are used.

☐ Overuse of words such as then, so, but, or, and as well as are avoided.

☐ Dead words are avoided.

☐ Unnecessary words are omitted.

☐ Spelling is correct.

☐ Writing is legible.

Pattern for a Cinquain

Writer's Notebook

Title

Line 1—One word (noun or name)

Line 2—Two adjectives describing Line 1

Line 3—Three verbs telling what Line 1 does

Line 4—Four words telling more about Line 1

Line 5—Word that means same as Line 1

Example:

Frosty

White, cold

Sitting, smiling, melting

On the snowy hillside

Snowman

Pattern for a Haiku

(Haiku are generally about nature.)

Title

Line 1—Five Syllables

Line 2—Seven Syllables

Line 3—Five Syllables

Example:

> Lovely butterfly
>
> Fluttering above the Earth.
>
> How fragile you are.

Pattern for a Tanka

(Tanka are generally about nature.)

Title

Line 1—Five Syllables

Line 2—Seven Syllables

Line 3—Five Syllables

Line 4—Seven Syllables

Line 5—Seven Syllables

Example:

> The moon shines brightly,
>
> Lighting the dark, dreary night
>
> With a pale, white light;
>
> Touching forests, mountains, seas,
>
> Giving brightness to the earth.

Pattern for a Couplet

Title

Line 1—Begin with descriptive word and add two items that fit description

Line 2—Something that rhymes with Line 1

Example:

> Beautiful mountains, rivers, and seas
>
> Are touched by the soft, summer breeze.

Pattern for a Limerick

Title

    Line 1—Three accented syllables

    Line 2—Three accented syllables; rhyme with Line 1

    Line 3—Two accented syllables

    Line 4—Two accented syllables; rhyme with Line 3

    Line 5—Three accented syllables; rhyme with Line 1

Example:

There was a young woman from Nance

Who loved to sing and to dance.

She attended a ball

At the palace hall

And soon was the pride of all France.

Writing an Ode

An ode can be either prose or poetry that is written about someone or something in honor of the subject. It usually speaks about that person or thing with respect and fondness; however, it can also speak in an amusing or satirical manner.

Example:

Ode to the End of Summer

Oh, Summertime you've come and gone.

I greatly anticipated your arrival.

I wanted you to linger on and on.

But, alas, now you are gone.

No longer shall I bask in your warm sun.

I shall find no joy in long days of fun.

Swimming, hiking, camping are all done.

The days grow short and the weather cools.

Fall awaits with autumn leaves.

The bright flowers of summer go to rest.

But memories shall linger.

Oh, the happy, carefree days of summer.

Writing Prompt:

Prompt: _____

Directions: _____

_____

_____

_____

_____

_____

_____

_____

_____

_____

_____

_____

_____

_____

_____

_____

_____

_____

_____

_____

_____